GW00739163

The Flourish Handbook

How to Achieve Happiness with Staying Power,
Boost your Well-being, Enjoy your Life More
and Reach your Potential

*A handbook for FLOURISHING
because THIS IS YOUR ONE AND ONLY LIFE!*

By Cheryl Rickman

*"The most important thing is to enjoy your life,
to be happy; it's all that matters,"*
Audrey Hepburn

First published in the USA by Createspace in 2013, an Amazon company

CreateSpace, a DBA of On-Demand Publishing, LLC.
100 Enterprise Way
Suite A200
Scotts Valley
CA 95066
United States

© 2013 Cheryl Rickman

The right of Cheryl Rickman to be identified as the author of this work has been asserted in accordance with the Copyright, Designs and Patents Act 1988.

Designed by Cheryl Rickman and Rochelle Mensidor

ISBN: 978-1-4912-4056-4

All rights reserved. No part of this publication may be reproduced, stored in a retrieval system, or transmitted, (other than for purposes of review) in any form or by any means, electronic, mechanical, photocopying, recording and/or otherwise without the prior written permission of the author. This book may not be lent, resold, hired out or otherwise disposed of by way of trade in any form, binding or cover other than that in which it is published, without the prior consent of the author.

Contents

Part 3 — Positive Relationships

Part 4 — Growth and Achievement

Dedication

For my mum and dad, Denise and Roger Rickman, who encouraged me to flourish, be grateful and work hard. I am grateful to have had them as my parents.

For my brilliant daughter Brooke Denise, herself a flourisher already who is my complete and utter sunshine. For my amazing mister, James for his patience, loyalty and support. For my wonderful supportive friends who shower me with love and encouragement.

May your belief in me enable others to flourish.

Introduction

••

What is Flourishing and Why Will It Improve Your Life?

"We must exercise ourselves in the things which bring happiness, since, if that be present, we have everything, and, if that be absent, all our actions are directed toward attaining it,"
Epicurus

Time flies. Fact! Time also (annoyingly) flies *faster* as we grow *older*. Often days, weeks, months, years blur into the next. As such, it is so incredibly important to get on with living a good, fulfilling life in which you flourish. It's important to create stand-out memorable moments and take time to remember and be thankful for those moments. It is also important to avoid ambling aimlessly from one day to the next without any sense of direction, meaning or purpose.

Then we can squeeze every ounce of pleasure from this life. Indeed, making the most of THIS ONE SHORT LIFE with which we have been blessed is what flourishing is all about: boosting our well-being to such an extent that we can get more from life, cope better with adversity, get more done and feel more in control.

And that's where this handbook comes in. ***The FLOURISH Handbook*** has been written to help you to flourish; to enable you to become the very best version of yourself and create the BEST LIFE that you can from this day forward. In doing so, you can become a better mum/dad, friend, wife, sibling, student, employee, boss, entrepreneur.... i.e. YOU, BUT HAPPIER ... A FLOURISHER; someone who has been enabled to flourish-ever-after.

So What Is Flourishing?

flour·ish
verb
❶ to be in a vigorous state; thrive: a period in which art flourished.
❷ to be in its or in one's prime; be at the height of fame, excellence, influence, etc.
❸ to be successful; prosper.
❹ to grow luxuriantly, or thrive in growth, as a plant.

Fortunately for you and I, there is a formula for flourishing; one that has been formulated, tried and tested by the best minds in positive psychology. These experts have discovered what they deem to be the blueprint for genuine, lasting happiness (not just fleeting feelings of joy, but happiness with staying power). It's called FLOURISHING and it has specific ingredients. You see, while happiness is something every human being strives for, happiness is merely a fleeting feeling. Flourishing is so much more than just a feeling – it is a way of being, a way of growing and a way of thriving.

**Flourishing is about more than simply *feeling* good,
it's about pursuing and experiencing a better life;
it's about building and optimising well-being.**

Once you know which elements make up well-being and focus on those areas, rather than focusing merely on happiness alone, you can live a rich, enjoyable and meaningful life with a high level of well-being.

The problem with happiness is that it's difficult to measure as it focuses predominantly on life satisfaction. Well-being, on the other hand, which flourishing creates, can be readily measured through the foundations on which it is built.

According to Martin Seligman, one of the forefathers of the flourishing concept, (who believes the word happiness is "so overused it has become almost meaningless") there are certain elements which comprise human flourishing. These include:

> "happiness, flow, meaning, love, gratitude, accomplishment, growth and better relationships."

Seligman and his team created a mnemonic to summarise these elements of flourishing after realising that, merely striving for and measuring happiness was not enough, and that measuring well-being was more helpful and fulfilling than measuring happiness.

Their catchword is PERMA. It stands for the **five measurable elements of well-being**, which are:

Positive Emotion
Engagement
Relationships
Meaning
Accomplishment

Happiness and life satisfaction are merely aspects of the *first* element of well-being – positive emotion. It is not enough to focus solely on that then. In order to flourish we must have:

❶ **POSITIVE EMOTION**: happiness and life satisfaction.
❷ **ENGAGEMENT**: engaged interest in our daily life, our learning and working activities which comes from using our skills, strengths and competencies to achieve a sense of 'flow' when we can lose ourself in an activity.
❸ **RELATIONSHIPS**: strong, supportive and rewarding social relationships.
❹ **MEANING**: a purposeful life which is valued, worthwhile and has meaning.
❺ **ACCOMPLISHMENT**: working towards and achieving goals and thus growing and developing.

Positivity pioneer, Martin Seligman, calls these the "five pillars of happiness". "Pretty much everything else is in service of one or more of these goals," says Martin. "That's the human dashboard." If we are able to tick these boxes, each creates a virtuous circle, each feeding the next... so that the more engagement and meaning our life has, the more likely we are to achieve our goals, which causes positive emotion, which makes us better able to build positive relationships, engage in our work, and so on and so forth.

Additionally, there are some notably positive side effects caused by these five elements. For instance, as we flourish we gain more vitality and resilience, which in turn gives us a heightened sense of optimism. As we gain control over our lives, bouncing back and forging forward as a result of flourishing, we build our self-esteem and self-determination. All of these feed into our well-being, boosting it further. Once we step on to the flourishing roller-coaster ride we embark on a self-fulfilling journey of growth and optimum well-being.

How Will This Handbook Enable You To Flourish?

No wonder that we all want to boost our well-being. Being content and happy is so evidently beneficial. Flourishers are, studies reveal, more productive, more able to build strong and meaningful relationships, more equipped to succeed and bounce-back from hardships. They are more optimistic, confident and happy; kinder, even healthier and more successful. This handbook aims to make it easier for everyone to flourish.

This handbook is broken down into four parts (bunching engagement together with meaning) across four quarters of the year to create an actionable tool which is highly practical and easy-to-digest.

What this handbook sets out to do then, is to help regular people, like you and me, to flourish. But, rather than merely read a book on the topic, this handbook equips you literally by giving you monthly tasks, daily actions and a GREAT BIG FLOURISH PLANNER into which you can schedule stuff that will enable flourishing within your daily life. Packed with exercises, quotes, reminders and monthly 'to do lists', this handbook will give you more control over YOUR ONE LIFE, reduce stress, boost your well-being and help you to navigate your way through the maze of life with its perpetual roller-coaster ride of ups and downs.

We all have the power to flourish; to create a better and happier life for ourselves by learning how to control our attitude, our mindset and the choices we make around recreational activities, work and relationships. Because you are like a seed. Just like a seed, you have all that you need within you to develop, to grow, to flourish.

Of course, we all have our default way of being; our 'status-quo-selves' if you like, and it can take more than reading a book to shift the way we behave/think/do things to positively impact our well-being. However, by *working* on our well-being and putting in some effort, we can make a real difference. Hence this HANDBOOK – a handy guide to take you on your journey to become a fully-fledged flourisher, i.e. someone who flourishes daily and, consequently has what it takes to experience long-lasting happiness, even during tough times, even when life throws you a curve-ball, because you will know how best to think, react and handle all that stuff.

This handbook will show you exactly how to flourish as you carry out exercises around gratitude, recollection, and constructive response. It will show you precisely how to de-clutter and enhance your environment and your mind power. It will help you to uncover your strengths and create a more meaningful and purposeful life in which you use them. It will take you on an illuminating and rewarding journey where you'll boost your well-being month-by-month over the course of a year. Rather than reading a book and trying to implement intentions all at once, this handbook gives you the opportunity to take one month at a time, step-by-step. No overwhelming scientific psychological jargon. Just focused intentions, backed up with research, plus practical tasks to complete each month which end with an easily-achievable to-do list at the end of each section.

Plus, access downloadable colourful versions of the worksheets and printable quotes which appear in this book at http://www.flourishhandbook.com/the-flourish-handbook-worksheets and enter the password: flourisherworksheets

You can then gradually build each intention and action into your whole way of being over time. The boxed out areas entitled FLOURISH PLANNER at the end of each month, summarise the ongoing tasks/actions that you will need to put into your planner going forward.

The aim of this book is essentially to help you to enjoy your life more. So that you feel happier, experience more joy, have more fun, have a more pleasant existence and equally feel less anxiety, guilt, envy, and so on. Optimising your well-being will have a knock on effect, making it easier for you to be patient, kind, thoughtful, generous and cheerful; making you more productive, energised and ultimately laying the foundations for you to achieve success in each area of your life.

Importantly, rather than just provide you with information, this handbook enables you to take purposeful action from the first exercise which asks you to de-clutter your home and workspace through to the ULTIMATE FLOURISH PLANNER which enables you to schedule fun and engaging activities, social events with positive people, purposeful work and specific goal-reaching and gratitude-based tasks into every single week.

While this handbook is a tool that you can use from this day forward to feel happier, enjoy your life more and get more done, it doesn't promise to obliterate down days from your life completely. We all have days when we feel a bit low, when we just can't be bothered. But, equipped with this tool, any down day will be decidedly more 'up' than it would have been BF (Before Flourishing). As such, even low days will be high-low days. With the wide variation of exercises, to-do-list tasks, practical pointers, guidance and 100-activities-to-flourish checklist, this handbook will essentially give you everything you need to flourish.

Born pessimists will not become optimists overnight. Some of our anxiety and misery and level of well-being is hereditary, just part of who we are – a given. However, we can still flourish and raise our level of well-being. There is no magic 'happy' book/pill/therapy... that will eradicate ALL blue feelings and down days, or that will cease all negative thoughts in their tracks forever so that you will live every minute of every day in complete and utter joy. Nope. We are human beings after all. Sometimes your efforts will go unrewarded, sometimes life will just be unfair yet, with the right preparation and knowledge, you can deal and cope with those thoughts/days/feelings of woe and you can come out on top; flourishing.

You can build these intentions and actions into your life gradually month-by-month and then keep doing them, behaving in this way, thinking accordingly... as a flourisher.

Why Is This Book Needed?

Let's face it. The world has become increasingly frowny. According to research, despite having so much more freedom, work-life balance and material gains than ever before (we can now instantly shop without leaving our houses, have our groceries delivered, afford more holidays) entire nations of people are generally no happier and in some cases **less happy** than they were 50 years ago.

In his book, *Flourish*, Martin Seligman explains:

"Denmark leads Europe with 33 percent of its citizens flourishing. The UK has about HALF THAT RATE, with 18 percent flourishing.... The hope that better externalities could make people lastingly happier was discouraged by a study of lottery winners, who were happier for a few months after their windfall, but soon fell back to their habitual level of grouchiness or cheerfulness. We adapt rapidly to windfall, job promotion, or marriage, so theorists argue, and we soon want to trade up to yet more goodies to raise our plummeting happiness. It we trade up successfully, we stay on the hedonic treadmill, but we will always need yet another shot."

And so, as we strive for a higher level of happiness and life satisfaction, as we set ourselves more goals and buy ourselves more stuff; as we continue to compare ourselves to others who appear better-off than us, we aren't getting any happier. Instead we, as nations, are getting more anxious and concerned and less fulfilled.

Through their work in education and defence, luminaries on the topic of well-being are tackling that issue by creating conditions to enable people to flourish. Martin Seligman is working with the military to develop strategies to prevent post-traumatic stress disorder (PTSD) and improve soldiers' psychological health. He is also, along with the likes of Richard Layard, director of the Well-being Programme at LSE's Centre for Economic Performance and author of *Happiness: Lessons from a New Science*, trying to encourage the teaching of well-being in schools.

Imagine if well-being lessons were part of the national curriculum. Entire nations could be lifted up to become better and happier human beings, living better lives, doing better in their jobs and creating a better economy. Flourishers outperform their unhappy counterparts. The better we feel, the more likely we are to be kind, helpful and creative; the more generous, light-hearted and effective we are. Conversely, when we feel low, we are more likely to lose interest, lose our temper, be defensive and cold-hearted. Happy people are healthier and friendlier, according to research. They make better friends, parents, citizens. Happy people are more productive, creative, helpful and resilient.

Imagine if every mother, teenager, MP and employer read this handbook? What a difference flourishers could make to world peace, saving the environment, boosting our economy and reducing crime. Or, at the very least, how much more patient and encouraging and kind we could all be?

For now though, let's start with YOU. Because, while happiness can be contagious as a mood, (via 'emotional contagion') you and only YOU are responsible for your own happiness. So let's give you all that you need to flourish. Ready? Excited? Then read on...

"If you want to have roses, it is not nearly enough to clear and weed. You have to amend the soil with peat moss, plant a good rose, water it, and feed it nutrients. You have to supply the enabling conditions for flourishing,"
Martin Seligman

Thrive. Develop. Grow.

Flourishing Audit

Grab a pen. Let's crack straight on and have a go at sussing out where you are right now so that you can assess whether you are flourishing or languishing in various areas of your life and see which areas to focus your time and attention on. Put a tick or a cross or a question mark after each of these:

I rarely worry about my past or future

I'm happy with what I have and often take time to consider how lucky I am

I never hoard things

My home is always spotless (not just when people are coming round) ;-)

I am organised, rarely late and never lose things

I have a strong sense of purpose in my life/work

I spend enough quality time with my children

I spend enough quality time with other members of my family

I always expect the best outcome

If something bad can happen it will happen to me

I have a good supportive circle of friends

I'm happy with what I look like

I rarely feel down in the dumps regardless of the time of day

I feel happier in the mornings and evenings than in the afternoons

I have more than enough time to do all I need to do each day

I have enough 'me-time' in my life to do activities that I enjoy

I often find time just to sit and be mindful

I am rarely stressed out or inpatient

I rarely argue

I am always nice to my parents/siblings

I often venture outside my comfort zone

I have many hobbies

I am in a wonderful relationship which is right for me

I love what I do work-wise and get excited about work

I know what I want and how I am going to get it

My dreams, goals and vision are very clear and I'm pursuing them

I get enough sleep and am mentally alert and full of energy

I am a patient and calm person

I get enough exercise and am physically fit

I am true to myself, always

I love my body

I eat a well-balanced healthy and nutritious diet

I regularly plan my meals

I am always aware and notice what's going on around me

I believe I'll be rewarded for my efforts

I always look on the bright side

I find it easy to forgive and rarely hold grudges

I find it easy to bounce back from tough times

Underline the areas which have crosses next to them. This could be about your body, sleep and exercise, perhaps your relationships with family and your relationship with your past? By auditing your life, and then taking the time to read this book, do the monthly tasks and complete the exercises, you can seize control over your own one and only life and feel alive, happy, grateful for what you already have and excited about what you will have in the future, as you make the necessary changes and FLOURISH.

Part 1

Positive Emotion (Happiness)

The Feel Good Factor: How To Create and Savour Positive Emotion

"Positive emotion does much more than just feel pleasant; it is a neon sign that growth is under way, that psychological capital is accumulating,"
MARTIN SELIGMAN

Cheerful feelings are fleeting. Until recently, happy feelings (happiness) were viewed as the ultimate goal to strive for. Yet flourishing is about more than just how we *feel*. That said, we still need to feel good and that is why positive emotion (happiness) is a vital ingredient in the flourishing pie.

There are a multitude of ways to induce happy feelings. Apart from experiencing special milestones, such as getting married or giving birth, we can shift our thinking and behaviour in a certain way and make specific changes to our lives that will make us feel happier more often. If we focus our attention each day on taking these actions and fulfilling these intentions we can boost our well-being tremendously and make those fleeting feelings of happiness last longer. Flourishing is, in essence, happiness with staying power. And so, this first section of the book shall focus on creating and savouring that positive emotion – the first 'pillar of flourishing'.

So hand over the first quarter of this year, the first three months, to building happiness, to creating and savouring positive emotion by de-cluttering your home and mind and boosting your energy. First, we'll do something practical by de-cluttering, enabling and enhancing your outer environment. Next we'll focus on YOU, on generating more mental and physical energy so that you are best placed to tackle the final part of the positive emotion pie – your mind. In month three we'll focus on de-cluttering your mind and enabling yourself to think more positively more regularly.

"It is not what happens to you,
but how you react to it that matters."
Epictetus (AD55)

Our reactions determine our mood. Each trial, tribulation and tragedy; each obstacle, hurdle and challenge that we face makes us either bitter or better, it either makes or breaks us. How you interpret external events and respond to stress will determine your level of positive emotion. So you have a choice - whether to become the victim or the victor. Which are you?

Those who learn how to control their reactions and thoughts are better positioned to experience happiness. People who have suffered great loss and tragedy have still found happiness by seeing things in a way that enables well-being, by finding a clarity of purpose which enriches life. By becoming a master of your own destiny and optimising the experiences you live throughout life, you will enjoy the journey. By interpreting everyday experiences in the right way you'll achieve an inner harmony that will give you the freedom to enjoy life, to love life and to experience deep joy.

Chapter 1

MONTH ONE:
Create an Enabling
Environment

Our outer world affects our inner world. So what better way to start on this flourishing journey than to roll our sleeves up and get our hands dirty? It's time to get stuck in and create a more enabling environment.

LOOK AFTER YOUR SPACE:
De-clutter and De-stress

1. **De-clutter.** Mess is oppressive. Clutter creates stress. Remove the burden of clutter and you'll remove some of the stress, thus providing more mental energy. Furthermore you'll save masses of TIME (with everything in its place and easier to locate). According to research, de-cluttering can reduce housework by 40 percent. (Back of the net!) It'll restore your mental energy and give you back space and time. It's incredibly uplifting too. Yippeeeee! Make room for what matters and give yourself more breathing (and living) space.

   - **Sort through your wardrobe.** Be ruthless. Ditch anything you haven't worn for over a year, even stuff you hope to fit into one day. You'll find you have more to wear as the good stuff will come out of hiding and the unwearable will be thrown away.

   - **Use good stuff now** (fine china, photo frames, and so on). There's no point saving all the good stuff you have in case the day never comes. Life is just too short.

- **Tackle the "dump zones".** These include the dining table, kitchen side, stairs, and so on.

- **Create specific places for specific things.** Then put stuff in the same place so you know where to find it. For example, keys. Put them in the same place every time you come in the door. This simple action will reduce stress induced by running late and having to leave 'now' yet being unable to do so due to lost keys. Gah! Anything that doesn't have a home, put it in a clutter bucket to deal with later.

- **Find better ways to organise your stuff.** This could involve buying new paperwork files or storage boxes or organising 'the drawer' (we all have one) in a hierarchy of importance with least important stuff at the back (rather than bunging everything into 'the drawer' haphazardly then wasting time rummaging in it from then on).

- **Stay on top of clutter.** Devote ten minutes every day from this day onward either mid-afternoon (if doing the school run) or early evening (after tea) to tidying. That way you are not greeted by the need to tidy in the morning. Also schedule in a 15-30 minute weekly slot to deal with paperwork and file it (*include this tidying time in your planner). Additionally, each time you leave a room, take an item back to its rightful place.

- **Get rid of whatever you don't need.** Give stuff that you don't need to people who might. Try Colleen Madsen's approach to de-cluttering and sell, give or throw away at least one thing per day over the course of one year. In doing so you'll own 365 less items.

2. **Enhance your environment.** Once you've taken a key source of stress (clutter) away and have organised your space, you

can work on making the most of what you are left with and add some simple touches to motivate you each time you enter that environment.

- **Set a budget.** Whether it's £10 or £100, set a budget to enhance where you spend most of your time, at home or work; to make it serene, inspiring or welcoming – whatever vibe you wish to create. For example, you might purchase a new pillow or cushion, a comfortable chair or lamp? Or how about an aromatherapy candle, picture frame or notebooks? For me, buying finely made luxury notebooks and fine tip coloured 'Uniball Eye' pens, i.e. the tools of my trade, gives me an incredible boost and makes my work more pleasurable. Additionally I now buy flowers once every two weeks with the money that I used to spend on magazines and newspapers. I subscribe to one magazine only and stopped reading newspapers due to the volume of upsetting news.

Note: I am not advocating retail therapy for the sake of it because I know that, while buying new stuff does boost happiness, it only does so temporarily. This is what's known in psychology circles as the 'hedonic treadmill' and stepping onto that treadmill means that instant gratification reduces the pleasure of anticipation which saving and planning create, and the novelty of our purchases wear off incredibly quickly. Your aim here is to only spend money on items that will improve the environment in which you spend the majority of your time (thus creating a long-lasting positive effect).

- **Make your environment smell nice.** Walking into your home and being greeted by a lovely subtle aroma is smile-inducing. Lavender and vanilla, for example have many well-being enhancing properties. They both soothe stress and lift mood.

- **Light it right.** We need light in our lives to enable us to look on the bright side. Keep that bright side burning bright with 60-11 watt daylight bulbs (otherwise known as happy light bulbs'). Try www.enviro-lights.co.uk. The American Psychiatric Association, among others, claims that exposure to bright light can improve your mood. It makes sense. Dingy rooms feel heavy and depressing to me whereas light generates a more pleasant and happier brain chemistry. Indeed, sufferers of SAD (Seasonal Affective Disorder) which affects 2 million people in the UK and Ireland and over 12 Million people across Northern Europe, find exposure to lightboxes via light therapy particularly useful. Lack of light causes an increase in the production of Melatonin (the hormone that makes us sleepy at night), and a reduction of Serotonin, the lack of which causes depression. The exposure to bright light therapy reverses the process. It's also important to set up your working area close to natural sunlight and get outside as often as you can during the day.

- **Decorate**. Colour can enhance mood. For example, yellow is well-documented to lift-spirits, while violet can enhance serenity (Leonardo da Vinci declares that meditation power can be increased ten-fold by meditating under gentle rays of Violet, as found in Church windows.) I try to buy yellow flowers or put flowers in yellow or purple vases.

- **"Dress like it matters,"** advises Richard Templar in his *Rules of Life* book. You will be more able to do this once you have freed up space in your wardrobe for the wearable clothes and bagged up the rest. I used to dress like it mattered as a teenager but, as the years have flown past, I no longer do so. Haven't done for some time. It's easier not to. It's easier to throw on some comfortable albeit scruffy joggers, a hoody (with or without coffee stain) scrape my hair back and get on with my busy day. I have generally opted for comfort over style. When I go out I always wear flat shoes as I don't wish to hamper my enjoyment of the experience, but I still aim to look my best. However, when I entirely eliminate style from the equation and go for 100% comfort, while I feel nice, I don't feel as self-confident (more self-conscious). So I get Richard's point. As such, during the process of writing this book I have bought some new clothes and am dressing each day like it matters. And guess what? It does make me feel better. I have chosen a style (brightly coloured skinny jeans or patterned leggings, floaty blouses, t-shirts or shirts, long cardigans and boots). I make sure the comfort quotient is still reasonably high, but I get the style/comfort balance right and make more of an effort on my appearance. You don't have to be a girly girl to do that. Who knew?

To Do List

To Do

• De-clutter
• Shop — smellies
    — lightbulbs
    — stuff (vase, flowers, cushions, frames)
• Decorate

FLOURISH PLANNER (ongoing)

Devote 15-30 minutes to tidying each day to stay on top of clutter/paperwork/keep spaces clear and organised.

Printable Quotes... to cut out n stick up

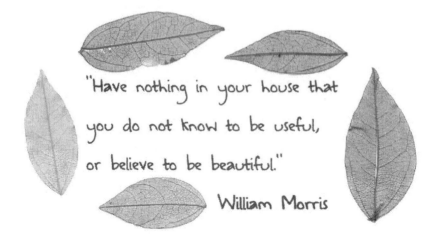

"Have nothing in your house that you do not know to be useful, or believe to be beautiful."

William Morris

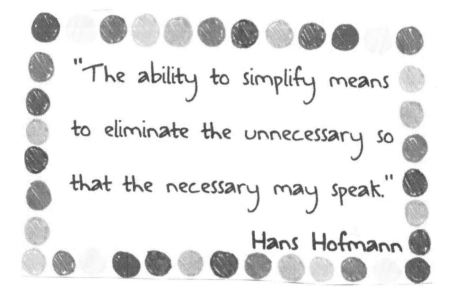

"The ability to simplify means to eliminate the unnecessary so that the necessary may speak."

Hans Hofmann

Chapter 2

MONTH TWO:
Generate More Energy

LOOK AFTER YOU!
Sleep, Exercise, Eat, Relax and Play

There is a definite link between ENERGY and well-being. Happiness is energising in itself. And it works the other way too. The more energy you have, the better you feel about yourself and the more able you are to get stuff done, participate, and stay motivated. Fundamentally, energy and well-being feed each other in a perpetual circle of glee. The more energy you have, the more able you are to engage in activities that boost-well-being. The more energy you have, the more self-control and self-mastery you have too, so you are better able to resist temptation, avoid procrastination and get on with your life. Energy boosts self-esteem and confidence as well. Conversely, if we are lacking in energy and feel tired, we tend to mill about aimlessly and feel overwhelmed by tasks that would usually make us feel good. Indeed, everything becomes so much more arduous when we lack energy. As such, energy-boosting should become a primary focus in your journey to improve your well-being, and that is the focus for this month.

"Energy is eternal delight,"
William Blake

1. **Get more sleep (go to bed earlier).** The recommended number of hours sleep we should all get per night is between seven to eight hours. Not easy if you have young children or are self-employed and work from home in the evenings.

Yet, just one extra hour of sleep per night (ideally before midnight) could dramatically and positively affect your well-being. In fact, you will struggle with many of the intentions, exercises and activities in this book if you are too tired, so try to make this intention a priority.

- Make your room dark. Turn off the light.
- Go to bed to sleep rather than to read/watch TV.
- Stop working at least one hour before you go to bed.
- Get ready for bed well before you get under the covers (I often find the process of teeth-brushing and flossing wakes me right up).
- Stretch before you get into bed.
- Say thank you for the good things that happened today.
- Imagine it's time to get up (that should automatically make you feel sleepy) ... zzz

2. **Get more exercise. Get active and get fit.** As well as giving you more energy, exercise releases endorphins which make you feel good AND think more clearly. Being active enhances your mood, your ability to engage and your ability to experience positive emotions. It's not about reducing fatness, it's about increasing fitness. Did you know that fit yet fat people halve their health risks simply by getting fit, however heavy they might be. So just move more.

- **Devote a month to finding your ideal exercise by trying different forms and classes**, whether on your own or in pairs (cycling, running, swimming) or a group activity (Bodyjam, Zumba, Netball)... pick up the phone and enrol in some classes. Try things out. Which activity makes you feel happiest and most energised?

- **Block book that exercise activity for the next month/term.** Commit to get more energy. <u>Note</u>: you should exercise for the feel good factor rather than for weight loss ('sanity not vanity'). Losing weight is just an added bonus.

- **Exercise on Mondays and Fridays at the very least.** It's a great way to start and end the week. Even a brisk 15 minute walk on a Monday morning will boost your energy and reduce stress. I walk the long way home from dropping my daughter at school on Monday morning and attend Bodyjam classes on Friday mornings. Three times a week I now also try to fit in 15 minutes of prancing around to an online exercise video or brisk walking when I feel at my lowest ebb (around 2.30pm). That gives me 30 minutes before the school run to do some household chores in a better mood than I used to (or have another burst of writing work).

- **Take energetic exercise breaks at the right time.** According to BRAC (Basic Rest and Activity Cycle) the average person is most alert, optimistic and energised in the late morning and mid-evening. This is when I find I write my best work. Around the middle of the afternoon and early hours of the morning we become more pessimistic and at our lowest ebb. (Somewhat morbidly, people tend to die at the bottom of their BRAC with more people dying in mid afternoon/early morning hours than any other time). So, to make the most of your natural cycle, you should aim to get physically active whilst at the bottom of your BRAC. For example, at 2.30pm or 3pm go for a brisk walk, dance to music*, partake in some form of exercise, even if just for a 15 minute burst. Having this 'energy break' enables better learning, teaching, thinking and more productive working thereafter. (*Researchers have revealed that an elevating piece of vibrant music enhances alertness, memory and attention levels as well as boosting our mood).

- **Create a list of gloom-banishing energising activities** that you can do and places that you can visit during those low ebb times at the bottom of your BRAC. For example, I've learned that if I do one of the following: take a shower, visit the library, go for a walk in 'my field', or dance, I keep that glum feeling at bay and

My 'Chin Up Buttercup' List
Things to do when I'm feeling fed up

- Go for a walk in the fields yonder
- Visit the library
- Listen to Daft Punk (loudly)
- Phone P or J for a natter
- Wallow in a hot bubble bath or shower
- Look at photos of my daughter
- Bounce on her trampoline
- Eat fruit salad with ice cream and maple syrup (one of my five a day in a very yummy way)
- Bake a cake or loaf of bread
- Do a 15 minute stint in the garden

My 'Chin Up Buttercup' List

Things to do when I'm feeling fed up

-
-
-
-
-
-
-
-

REPLACE GLOOM WITH BLOOM :-) Note: See Chapter Five on Engagement for a list of activities that you can pick n mix to boost your well-being and replenish your zest for life; whether that's walking, meditating, dancing or escaping in the pages of a novel. Suss out what you need to do to invigorate your emotional energy when you feel depleted.

- **Stand on your head.** Doing so not only improves brain function if you do it regularly, MRI studies also reveal that headstands can improve your mood and release stress (unless you have a stress-headache).

- **Walk more.** Step into the light (so to speak). Walking is an immediate mood-booster, stress-reducer and energiser. Furthermore, walking gives you TIME TO THINK (and think with more clarity due to the chemicals that the brain releases when you walk – an added bonus). It's recommended that we walk for 10,000 steps per day. To see how you fare, get a pedometer. Natural daylight improves mood too, so walking outside is a veritable serotonin and dopamine inducing treat.

"All truly great thoughts are conceived while walking,"
Nietzsche

3. **Eat healthily.** Research has revealed that what you eat can have a major impact on your mental well-being because food affects how you feel as well as impacting your physical health. Healthy eating can boost your energy level and enhance your mood by positively altering your metabolism and brain chemistry.

- **Pick and mix from this list of highly recommended FEEL GOOD MOOD-BOOST FOODS:** Blueberries, almonds, spinach, tuna, oranges, bananas, sweet potatoes, brown rice, avocado, brazil nuts, sardines, oats, lentils, chicken and turkey, water, yoghurt, dark chocolate, oysters.

Replace sugary snacks with blueberries or almonds where possible.

- **Eat (and drink) more fruit and veg.** Get a juicer and schedule juicing. I have done exactly this so that on arrival home from school my daughter and I get juicing before sitting down to sip our juice and have a nice calm chat. More fruit n veg, some quality time and replacing the request for sugary snacks with natural sugar = triple win. Aim for anti-oxidant rich berries and veggies. And eat more apples. Visit www.juiceproducer.com for some great juicers.

- **Plan your meals.** Use this special **Flourishers Feel Good Food Menu**, kindly contributed by nutritionist, Priya Tew of www.dietitianuk.co.uk

<u>5 Day Healthy Meal Planner</u>

Each day contains 2-3 portions of calcium containing foods
At least 5 portions of fruit and vegetables
Carbohydrates correctly portioned at each meal
Balanced snacks
Nutritious protein sources
Wholegrains

Breakfast	Snack	Lunch	Snack	Dinner
Porridge made with 35g porridge oats, semi skimmed/ skimmed milk topped with 1 tbsp sultanas and chopped fresh fruit	30g mixed nuts and seeds with 3 dried apricots.	2 slices of wholemeal toast topped with 200g baked beans and plenty of chopped salad. 1 low fat yoghurt.	2 jaffa cakes and 1 banana.	120g fillet of fresh cod with 50g prawns, a handful of baby spinach and a splash of skimmed milk, wrapped in foil and baked. Serve with half an avocado and sliced tomatoes plus 3 egg sized potatoes.
2 slices of wholemeal toast with 2 scrambled eggs plus 2 grilled tomatoes.	150g fat free Greek yoghurt and 1 handful of berries.	Carrot and Lentil soup served with 1 granary roll and 30g cheese.	2 oatcakes topped with low fat soft cheese and cucumber.	75g dried pasta, cooked and and served with a low fat tomato sauce, 100g chicken and plenty of vegetables.

Breakfast	Snack	Lunch	Snack	Dinner
40g of a wholegrain cereal topped with fresh fruit and served with milk.	Home-made flap-jack http:// www.di-etitianuk. co.uk/2012 /01/28/no-fat-no-sug-ar-super healthy-oaty-bars/	1 tortilla wrap stuffed with 80g roast chicken pieces, shredded lettuce, cucumber, tomato and 1 tbsp mango chutney.	Smoothie made with 100g natural yoghurt, 1 banana, 1 handful mixed berries, 1 tsp cinnamon, a dash of lemon juice and a splash of milk.	Chilli and rice, made with 90g lean beef mince, chopped tomatoes, fresh herbs, a splash of red wine, tomato puree, onion, garlic, 2 tbsp kidney beans and chilli. Serve with 75g cooked rice and a mixed salad.
2 slices of wholemeal toast topped with peanut butter. 1 glass of orange juice and 1 low fat yoghurt.	1 apple with 25g nuts.	2 slices of wholemeal bread, a thin spread of spread filled with 45g tuna, sweetcorn and cucumber. Fruit and low fat rice pudding.	30g cheese served with 2 large rice cakes and 1 tbsp chutney plus 6 cherry tomatoes.	Mushroom Risotto made with half fat creme fraiche and served with a green salad.

Breakfast	Snack	Lunch	Snack	Dinner
50g no added sugar muesli with 1 chopped banana and served with yoghurt or milk.	Raw vegetables with 1 tbsp low fat hummus.	Chicken salad made with 80g chicken, salad leaves, chopped carrots, cucumber, peppers, and sweetcorn, dress with a low fat salad dressing. Serve with 3 new potatoes.	Homemade popcorn (2 handfuls) with a glass of fruit juice.	Roast a mix of courgettes, peppers and mushrooms in 1 tbsp olive oil for 30 minutes. Cook 75g dried pasta. Mix the roasted vegetables into the pasta along with 50g low fat mozzarella cheese and some freshly chopped herbs.
2 wheat bisks with sliced melon, strawberries, 1 tbsp chopped nuts and milk	Sliced raw vegetables with 1 tbsp salsa and 1 tbsp low fat soft cheese.	1 wholemeal pitta bread with 2 tbsp low fat hummus, sliced peppers and spinach leaves. 1 reduced fat packet of crisps and a handful of grapes.	1 yoghurt topped with 1 tbsp crunchy granola.	Jacket potato with 100g tuna, dressed with 1 tbsp low fat mayo served with rocket, sliced raw carrots, celery, walnuts and apple.

- **Drink more water.** I have put 'drink water' on my schedule ever hour from 9am til 3pm. It doesn't work, I don't drink water on the hour every hour, but three or four times a day I remember and, subsequently drink 50% more water than I used to. Bonus!

4. **Relax.** Give yourself a break and plan some me-time space. Care for you. Devote 15-30 minutes (minimum) to yourself every single day. If you cannot realistically do that, which is not uncommon, give yourself some me-time every other

day at the very least. You are the chief of your own life. So it makes sense to give yourself some time to yourself. Time to recharge, refresh and relax.

- **Do ABSOLUTELY NOTHING with no interruptions**. This 'doing nothing – just being with yourself' can take place outside (sitting in the garden, walking down a lane) or inside (sitting on the sofa, laying in the bath). Try to clear your mind of thoughts or, if you find that near impossible, focus on motivating happy thoughts. Pure you-time. (See page 146 for more information about meditation and stilling your mind).

- **Practice DIY reflexology and stimulate your adrenal glands**. By massaging your palms you can de-stress. Simply use your thumb to massage the base of the other thumb (the palms chakra point).

5. **Play**. Be creative or tap into your creativity by appealing to your senses and being playful.

- **Listen to music.** Dance round the room or tap your foot. Whether you stay still while you listen or get active, the very act of listening to music is one of the most effective and quickest way to improve your mood and boost energy. Music has the power to energise, exhilarate and relax us. Consequently music triggers happiness by stimulating the brain. This is why some hospitals play music to patients during medical procedures in order to keep them calm and reduce anxiety, blood pressure and heart rate. Take some time to get blissed out via music. *Visit* http://www. youtube.com/playlist?list=PLLa4kbM0s54NnG2otwn_ IxHqVURZP7gp1 *to listen to The Flourishers Music Playlist.*

- **Play games to ignite your imagination and boost your well-being**. Take a look at http://janemcgonigal.com/ play-me/ which features alternate reality games designed to improve real lives and make players happier in their everyday lives (by dancing more or being kinder) or solve real problems (such as climate change and global peace). Jane aims to design games which tap into the science of positive psychology and so build stronger social relationships, serve a purpose, provide engagement and explore a full range of positive emotions.

- **Scribble and doodle.** Do some colouring in (with or without your children). Karen Salmansohn suggests doodling hearts with smiley faces. She says, "The silliness of this doodling action combined with the repeated visual stimuli of seeing icons representing love will cheer you up." This is especially effective if you then give your heart doodles to a loved one, cheering them up in the process.

And finally... you can gain energy from a surprising place:

6. **Just get on with it.** Do that task you've been neglecting. I know. Meh! You don't really want to, but you WILL feel good once it's done, energisingly good. It will no longer niggle you, so your mind will be clearer to allow more happy feelings in and your mind will be lifted as a direct consequence of just getting that thing DONE. Put this book down and do it now, QUICK... go on, before you change your mind.

To Do List

MORE
Sleep

MORE
Excercise

Eat healthier
Juice stuff
Drink more water

CHILL
PLAY
SCRIBBLE

Do THAT
pesky task

FLOURISH PLANNER (ongoing)

Schedule in:
- Early nights at least three nights per week (and stick to them)
- Drinking water every hour on the hour (you won't but you will drink more than you do now as a consequence).
- Exercise (classes, 15 minute bursts at the bottom of your BRAC, walking sessions, etc).
- Meal planning time. (I tend to do mine before I do my online grocery shop).

Printable Quotes... to cut out n stick up

"Energy and persistence conquer all things."

Benjamin Franklin

- ✂

"The higher your energy level,

the more efficient your body.

The more efficient your body,

the better you feel and

the more you will use your talent

to produce outstanding results."

Tony Robbins

Chapter 3

MONTH THREE:
Harness Your Mind Power

Boost Your Emotional Energy

In order to survive, thrive and sustain a zest for life on a daily basis we need two kinds of energy. We need **physical energy** which nutritious food, sleep and exercise provide us with, and we need **emotional energy.** It is the latter which we'll cover in this Chapter. According to Mira Kirshenbaum, a US psychotherapist and author of T*he Emotional Energy Factor,* 70% of our energy requirements are emotional with only 30% of our energy requirements physical. "It's the emotional component we need to face challenges, to have hope, to be able to respond with interest and excitement to an opportunity," says Kirshenbaum.

In this day and age our get-up-and-go can be dramatically affected by overwhelm; by taking on too much and trying to live up to unrealistic expectations that we place on ourselves or are placed on us by others. The feelings of guilt and perfectionism work against us. When we feel that we are not living up to our own or others' expectations we feel emotionally depleted and fatigued. These guilt-ridden feelings sap our emotional energy and thus, our zest for life. To combat this, as well as sourcing feel-good activities that replenish our resources and recharge our batteries we need to focus on our mind and give ourselves a break. There are various practical ways to do this and it need not be to drop the amount of stuff or people in your life (as reducing your commitments can create a less rewarding life) – instead you should focus on what you think about and how you think so that you can focus on what serves you well and bolster your resilience.

1. **Assess your thought patterns and define what makes you feel good or bad.** Only then can you make the right choices about what you devote your thoughts to and eliminate the thoughts and activities that deplete your emotional energy. In doing so you can de-clutter your mind and focus on the positive thoughts and empowering beliefs that enable you and boost your energy, rather than focusing on negative restrictive and limiting beliefs that disable you and sap your energy.

   - **Keep a thought diary to audit emotional energy.** List thinking patterns that boost your energy and sap your energy. For example, dwelling on a certain person's behaviour, worrying about finances or feeling jealous about how Facebook friends seem to have what you want... all of these can sap your emotional energy. Conversely, when you think about an activity with a person you are looking forward to seeing, say 'no' to something you really don't want to do, or decide to please yourself rather than other people, you are likely to feel that your emotional energy is boosted.

     Once you've listed these thoughts, think about ways to reduce the energy-sapping stuff and increase the energy-boosting stuff. For example, when you feel yourself dwelling on someone's behaviour. Notice your thought process. Stop. Focus with intent on thinking about something else or doing something that requires your full concentration or simply take some deep breaths. Do whatever it takes to move your thinking away from those energy-sapping thoughts. (We'll be covering Mindfulness in Chapter 6).

     If you are worried about your finances, tackle the problem head on. Find ways to increase your income or reduce your outgoings; compare tariffs and change utilities and insurance providers – take action and you'll feel better.

Do nothing and you won't. And, if you feel like you are constantly comparing yourself to people on Facebook or your siblings, take some time to list what you have. Chances are you have a lot of what other people would like, whether you can see that or not. If you can't flip the balance towards being grateful for what you have or can't see that the person you envy may be presenting a self-edited version of their lives which doesn't include the less rosy stuff, then spend less time on Facebook or around people who make you feel inadequate, then tackle the problem and focus on approving of yourself and taking action to achieve what you wish for. There are many confidence-boosting activities peppered through this handbook and a goal-achieving-action-plan in Chapters 8 and 9. If looking forward to doing things with certain people in your life makes you feel good, plan to do more of those things with those people. (There's more about spending time with feel-good people - your 'positive peeps' in Chapter 7). In short, whatever is enabling or disabling you to feel good, you can do something about it.

Thoughts 'n stuff which make me feel bad

Thoughts 'n stuff which make me feel good

2. **Bolster your resilience.** This all comes down to how you react in times of adversity. Resilience is the ultimate key to 'psychological/emotional fitness'. As Nietzsche famously said, "What does not kill me makes me stronger." And it does. It truly does. After coming out the other side of a crisis or traumatic period in your life, you may find that you are better prepared to deal with situations or relate to certain people; you may become better equipped to give guidance and support to others, you may even become a better wife or husband or parent as you appreciate them more than ever. You may find you are better able to prioritise, have a better understanding, spot more opportunities and have more of a zest for life. And, when you realise that you have changed positively as a result of your crises, that bolsters your resilience even more as you realise that something good came from something bad. You realise that, even if the worst does happen, you will be all right. You will even grow into a better, stronger version of yourself. This knowledge enables you to grow and, of course, to flourish.

- **Audit your resilience strategies, strengths, resources and experiences.**

  - What do you do to reduce stress and boost your emotional energy? What are your strategies? Do you go for a run, listen to music, take a shower?
  - What are your strengths of character which make you feel proud to be you? (You may be particularly driven and passionate, kind or friendly, for example).
  - Who do you rely on to support you when you are feeling emotionally wrung out?
  - What have you learned about yourself from how you have coped in the past with challenges, obstacles and tragedies?
  - How do you react when something bad happens to you? Do you expect more bad things to happen and feel helpless? Or do you feel determined to fight it

or not let it happen again? Do you feel that it is just part of the journey, the rollercoaster of life, which comes with downs as well as ups and just get on with things? Or do you catastrophize and worry about the worst case scenario? If you do the latter, try putting things into perspective whenever you experience intense worry or fear about something. Consider the worst case scenario, as you already have done, then consider the best case scenario, and then the most likely case scenario. Learning to put things into perspective enables you to breathe, assess and continue in a resilient manner.

The answers to these questions will show you that you do already have what you need to be resilient and cope with whatever life throws at you. And, if there are areas which you feel are weaker than others (for example your family may live miles away so your support network may need some attention, or you may feel that you need to learn some new skills) then spend a bit of time working on strengthening those areas to boost your resilience. Go on courses, read books, contact old friends and make new ones. Do whatever is necessary to fill those gaps.

Note: See Chapter Six on Mindfulness – a veritable calming and resilience boosting strategy.

Resilience Audit

To reduce stress/boost my emotional energy I tend to (refer to your Chin Up Buttercup list on pages 33-34 if you like):

Characteristics/strengths that make me proud to be me. I am:

Resilience resource. Supportive people I rely on in my life include:

What have I done in the past that proves my resilience? How did I cope with the worst situations I've dealt with? What did I do? What can I learn from that?

LOOK AFTER YOUR HEAD:
De-Clutter and Focus Your Mind

Scientific research tells us that a proportion of our happiness level is predetermined by various factors including genetics, gender, age, marital status, income, health and various other circumstances with between 30-40 per cent of our happiness determined by **how we think and act.** This means that, while we have an inbuilt 'happiness range' created by genetics and circumstances, we can dictate whether we push the predetermined genetic range to its uppermost or lowest limit, and we can do that through our **thoughts** and our **actions**.

> *"True happiness isn't about the THINGS you have;*
> *it's about the THOUGHTS you have.*
> *That's why it's called positive THINKING not positive THING-ING."*
> **Karen Salmansohn**

There is a "science bit" behind the "you are what you THINK about all day long" notion: our unconscious mind has a lot of responsibility in creating our current reality and our future. And that part of our mind tends to find it easier to access the thoughts that have most recently or most frequently been thought about. For example, if you focus your thoughts on positive things, such as gratitude for what you have and goals you'd like to reach, your unconscious can easily access them and, in doing so, can work to create good feelings, motives and judgements that are fed to your conscious mind.

The law of attraction (the belief that "like attracts like") also suggests that we attract into our lives all that we think about. If we think we can do something, we will be more likely to go ahead and do it than if we believe we can't, which will also become a self-fulfilling prophecy. If we focus on how much we dislike driving up the motorway to work or how much we dislike our job, we are likely to attract motorway closures and more reasons to dislike our job. If we spend the time that we are stuck in a traffic jam visualising ourselves working in our dream job and considering the elements of our existing lives which we are thankful for, we are more likely to attract a dream job offer or circumstances which enable us to realise our dreams than if we sit there cursing the traffic/job/other people.

The problem is, positive thinking is oh-so-easy to say but sometimes not so easy to do. Life gets in the way, other people's grumpiness brings us down. Our good intentions are so frequently diminished and we end up fighting a losing battle. And yet there are many ways to stay positive regardless of what is thrown at us on any given day.

This is a GINORMOUSLY BIG DEEP subject and, as such, this chapter is longer than the two prior ones. However, if you select to focus on one specific intention (the numbered parts) each day, you'll be able to tackle this topic in easily digestible chunks and will soon be able to face whatever is thrown at you and remain relatively unruffled regardless.

Learn From, Cherish, Then Let Go Of The Past

1. **Take some time to reminisce.** Happy moments can be maximised and amplified or minimised and curtailed. The amount of ATTENTION we give to each individual happy experience will determine whether that happy moment is amplified or ambushed. By first *anticipating* a happy event, *savouring* and enjoying it as it happens, then *expressing* and *recalling* that happy memory we amplify that magical moment. The recollection of happy moments focuses attention on them and therefore enhances them. Remembering happy times milks those moments for every last drop of joy available, so you can really get the most from each period of joy. Looking back at photographs which captured those happy times, sharing those photos with others, remembering and talking about happy memories -

all of these activities boost positive emotion and put you in a frame-of-mind for positive thinking. So today, do something that will better enable that reminiscing.

- **Keep memories alive and provide plenty of opportunities to relive them.** Doing so amplifies positive emotions. Take some time to do this. Get creative. You can CREATE:

  - Photo books via www.Photobox.com.
  - Memory boards to display on your walls.
  - New family traditions.
  - Filing boxes filled with memorabilia such as party invitations and cards.
  - Story scrap books of your 'family adventures'.
  - Family newsletters to distribute periodically (quarterly rather than annually).

2. **Leave the (not so happy) past behind.** *DISCLAIMER: This bit may make you sad before it makes you happy.* Just as dwelling on happy times intensifies positive emotion, so dwelling on sad times amplifies negative emotions. What we give our attention to comes to the surface for both our conscious and unconscious mind to access and magnify. So, while it's wise to focus on recollecting fond memories and moments, bad memories should be eliminated as much as possible. Of course, from time to time, something will remind us of a bad moment in our past or we will ruminate. So here's a bunch of ways to shift your attention away from the memories that don't serve you well which can (if you give power to them) diminish your happiness.

   - **Accept that you cannot change the past and that even negative events have shaped you in a positive way.** Write down three sad experiences that you no longer want to dwell on. Next to the event (death of a loved one, miscarriage, rejection...) write down any one or two positive lessons that it taught you about yourself (e.g. to appreciate what

I have today, that I am stronger than I thought I was, that I have incredibly supportive friends/loved ones, to persist because the next time may not result in rejection, and so on). This process in itself will bring back memories you may have successfully demoted to the back of your mind, which may seem counter-productive, being as I've just suggested that you leave unhappy memories behind and avoid dwelling on them. If they are too painful, feel free to leave this exercise out. However, giving those memories some small amount of air-time now, intentionally, and then dealing with the positives and strengths that those events have given you should be a cathartic exercise and, once completed, you will be better able to leave those events in the past where they belong.

Sad stuff that has happened	Positive stuff it taught meabout me
1.	
2.	
3.	

Here's the thing. What's done is done. You can't do anything about it. Accept this and you will be better equipped to move on. Embrace the stuff that has happened to you as character-forming, as necessary evils that have in fact boosted your strength and taught you something important. The clique 'what doesn't break you makes you stronger' is true, as all cliques generally are. But even stuff that *does* break you has a purpose; to make you stronger than you thought possible.

Downpours of rain happen so that we can cherish the sunshine and appreciate the blue skies when they appear. If everything was lovely all the time and life was easy, we wouldn't appreciate it and we wouldn't grow. We need the rain to flood us from time to time. If there was no struggle, there would be no joy of achievement. As such, it is important to try to cherish the rain too. When life is down, the only way is up. Defeat and misfortune provide us with an opportunity to develop and improve.

Life throws tragedy and loss, heartbreak and frustration at us sometimes. Life can be ridiculously unfair with moments which completely suck! Yet, in dealing with these moments and events as they happen and then choosing to let them go you will be better equipped to enjoy your life thereafter. The husband or wife who had an affair, the death of a parent, the unfair treatment at work --- rather than let these terrible events suck the positivity out of you and bubble away creating bitterness, resentment, anger, deep sadness and heartbreak creating a double loss (the event and now the negative feeling). Once we have succumbed to those feelings and look at what has happened and move on, we can look back and realise we are stronger because of those events.

You only get burdened with as much as you can carry. For example, my mum, Denise Rickman nee O'Farrell was one of those shiny happy people whose smile lit up a room. She was incredibly kind and thoughtful, always putting other people, (especially me, her only daughter) first. This was despite the fact that she was, on a daily basis, in immense pain. She suffered from the crippling disease Multiple Sclerosis and spent the last third of her life in a wheelchair. She joked with people that they could remember her name Denise as 'de knees on de legs' referring to her condition with good humour. Regardless of the pain she was in she never ever complained and, no matter how petty my problems were comparatively ('so and so doesn't like me anymore') she always listened, encouraged and offered love. She was an amazing and inspirational strong woman. And while she was outwardly smiling like a ray of sunshine, the fact that she'd been told she only had 10 years to live 20 years before possibly filled her internal thoughts with worry. She put a brave face on but inside this must have affected her.

My mother died aged 43 when I was just 17. Obviously this was an enormous blow to me. We were very close, although I had annoyingly been going through a rebellious teenage phase so wasn't being as nice to her as I had been in the preceding 15 years. I felt guilt, anger, sadness, incredible deep heart-wrenching pain at the unfairness of it all. Why her? Why me? Why now? She wouldn't see me graduate from my degree, or pass my driving test. She'd miss out on seeing me get married or have children of my own. She would never be a grandmother and would never meet my child. And I would never get to speak to her, cuddle her, or even see her again.

At the time, I was 17, I rebelled harder than I had been. I blamed my dad for not being able to deal with her disability even though I now realise it can't have been easy for him either. I felt sad and angry with the universe that my inspirational, strong and encouraging mum had been taken from me. How was that fair? I got the anger out of my system. I went entirely off the rails, while continuing to pursue my degree. But none of that helped because it just made me feel guiltier, knowing that my mum would be distraught to see me like that (although at least I hadn't dropped out of university and was still pursuing my goal of getting a job in the media - I'd been brought up well enough and had enough drive and determination to have not given up entirely).

And so, in my 20s I dusted myself off and pulled myself together. I couldn't forget some of the stuff that happened during my teenage years between my mother and father, but I chose to forgive; it was difficult for everyone. I chose to look at things differently. Yes, being a mum without a mum sucks, losing her isn't fair, not having her around to phone and chat with is heart-breaking – BIG TIME! (My friends now appreciate their mums so much more). But... I suddenly felt lucky. I was lucky to have had *her* – Denise Rickman – as my mother. What a blessing. She influenced me: my character, my choices, my life so greatly and so positively. She gave me determination and self-belief. She taught me about acceptance and strength and gratitude for what you have. She was incredibly patient, something I am still working on.

Someone gave me a poem, "smile because she has lived, don't cry because she has gone." Someone else told me not to cry because "she lives on within you, and she'll live on within your children and their children... she will never die." These statements helped.

Now, as a 38-year-old woman, with a 4 year old daughter (Brooke Denise) I admit that I do have the occasional "I just want my mum" deep dark sob. But, as time heals, I cry less. Moreover I feel genuinely blessed to have had my mum in my life, albeit for such a short time. I'm grateful for all that she was and all that she gave to me, which was much. And, if I can be half the mother she was, I'll be proud.

Now I choose not to dwell on my loss. Not to feel anger or that the world owes me anything. It doesn't. I am stronger as a result of my loss. I wish I hadn't had to lose my mum, but I have and I cannot change that. And so I have dealt with it, felt the various stages of grief and come out the other side as someone I hope my mum would be proud of. Because of that I can talk about it and have not blocked out the pain of loss. I have embraced it, moved on with my life and taken strength from that pain. I feel proud to have dealt with this period of my life. It could have broken me; it nearly did. But I didn't let it. And so I am stronger. And now, I watch my daughter playing happily and I feel so pleased and grateful and lucky to have her; I see some of my mother's characteristics in her and I teach her all about Nanny Denise from time to time. My daughter has partially filled the hole that loss left. I feel incredibly grateful for that.

The stuff I have gone through, the 'baggage' if you like, is no longer baggage. It's important because it makes me, well... me. It has shaped me into the person I am today.

I realised that forwards is the only way. There is little point in looking backwards because that's not the way I'm going. To quote Dory, the adorably forgetful fish in Finding Nemo: "Just keep swimming. Just keep swimming."

As this book was about to go to print, I was dealt another crushing and unfair blow, and so I must add in this paragraph to share the story. Just two months ago as I write this I was told that my dad had Mesothelioma (asbestos-lung-cancer). I was told it was terminal and there was no treatment. He had been given less than six months. I was, naturally, devastated, shocked and saddened. In fact, he actually had just three weeks to live after that terrible diagnosis. The strength I have needed to draw upon to cope with this has been tested. But I couldn't let it crush me.

I needed to be there for dad and remain strong for my daughter. I was so proud of how well he handled it, with such dignity. I am grateful to have had the knowledge so that I could spend time with him, tell him how much I love him – do all that I needed to to make him as comfortable as I could. I couldn't change his diagnosis. I couldn't do anything about it. All I could do was to make him comfortable, show him memories, give him my time, tell him how I felt about him; how glad I was that he's my dad. All I could do was feel blessed to have such incredibly supportive friends and family; feel pleased that he got to know my daughter, his grandaughter, and that they were able form a relationship over the past five years; feel thankful that we were warned what was round the corner so that we could try to prepare ourselves and express our love. I wish this didn't have to happen, but it has. All I could do was react to it in a way that made my dad feel proud and relieved that I would be ok.

My father passed away in the early hours of Fathers' Day 2013 just three weeks after discovering that he had a terminal disease (just over a month ago). I still can't believe that he too is gone and still feel shocked about how quickly this all happened. And yet the hardest battles are given to the strongest soldiers. I have chosen to let this loss strengthen me and do my dad proud rather than to let it break me or define me. We have lots of good memories of dad/grandpa and I still have so much in my life to be thankful for. I'm glad to have had him as my dad and I'm glad he took early retirement and got to travel the world over the last decade. Today I focus on flourishing, just as he would want me to.

The deepest pain is generally the the most empowering. Let things motivate and inspire and strengthen you rather than affect and squash and weaken you.

Think about it. Look back. You didn't think you could do it did you? But you did. You overcame those obstacles. You are still here and anyone who tried to bring you down; any situation or event that attempted to break you failed. You're still here, you're reading this book. You're ok! Nice work!

Do well. Don't dwell. Guilt is harmful. It doesn't change anything. It doesn't undo what has already been done. What it can do is make you feel so bad that you resolve never to do whatever it is you feel guilty about ever again. And that's great. Learn from mistakes, always. But then move on. The minute you've made that decision, that resolution to never treat someone in that way or do that kind of thing, push the guilt away, take a deep breath and move on, smiling that you've just made such a good and important decision.

The only good thing about guilt is that it reveals that you are a decent human, because bad people don't feel it. They don't care.

You do; hence the guilt. All you can do if you feel guilty if you have genuinely done something wrong, consider what you might do to put it right, then put it right, and move on. And, if it helps you release that guilt, write a letter to the person you feel you have wronged. You don't necessarily have to post it, but writing it will help. I wrote one to my mum to apologise for being a crap teenager. I could almost feel her saying, 'That's ok darling, I know it was just a phase. I love you. Always did. Always will.' And, when I had my daughter I realised I was forgiven because we will always love and forgive our children.

"You are the sum total of everything that has happened in your life. The successes and failures, the achievements and the mistakes. If you were to take any of the imperfect bits out of that equation, you wouldn't be you."
Richard Templar, *The Rules of Life*

- **Forgive. Let it go.** You may experience unjust events where someone copies you. They might copy your website word for word, they may do you some wrong, they may promise something and fail to deliver. You may be treated badly or witness someone else being treated badly. There are all sorts of wrongs that we need to rise above and forgive people for. Forgiving people, letting bygones be bygones is empowering. It gives you back the control of the situation. Forgive. Try it. Forgiveness feels good. We all make mistakes. That person who copied your website, over-promised, treated you wrongly, they made a mistake. They are probably not a bad person. End of.

- **Listen to your instinct and learn from your mistakes.** Follow your gut instinct. Stop yourself before ploughing ahead with a rash decision. Take a step back to get all of the information. Listen to you, the inner you, the all-knowing sometimes-sarcastic you which says 'Um. *Hello*? What on earth did you do *THAT* for?' or 'you can do better, try again' or 'oops, you should apologise' or 'Doh!' ;-) Heed it and try to do so before you take actions that you may regret. Tune in to it when making decisions. Because foresight is better than hindsight. You can only learn from mistakes. You can't undo what you did. Better to make the right choices ahead of acting. Instinct enables that.

- **Like yourself.** Accept who you are, warts and all. I'm not perfect, but I am me. And I quite like me actually. I've had moments when I haven't, when I've wished I was more like so-and-so, more this or more that. But now I'm in my late 30s I like me just the way I am. I accept I have weaknesses as well as strengths. I'm human. I enjoy my own company. I sometimes do things that make me cringe or feel silly and very imperfect indeed. But I am me and I accept that. I learn from mistakes I have made in the past. That's all I can do. I can't change what's done because it's done. Happened. Gone.

- The human being is a complex creature. And so, the only way to move forward, to be the best version of yourself, is to first accept who you are, warts and all, and develop and grow from that. Nobody is perfect or shall ever be. Even those who develop and grow and become the best version of themselves, do stuff they later regret with the benefit of hindsight, say the wrong thing, do the wrong thing... but hey... we are human and, just as we may have some irksome moments/ characteristics, we have a great deal to be thankful for. Most people are truly wonderful. Give yourself a break. Give yourself some praise and focus on the good; on your strengths, your abilities and accept everything that makes you YOU.

I like me because I am:

Think Positive and Act Happy

Complaining, criticising, blaming or just being plain grumpy means you are not being grateful. Genuine heart-felt gratitude empowers and transforms lives (more on that in Chapter Eight). Each time you feel yourself slipping into a huff, being critical of others or simply complaining about something rubbish that has happened. Stop and think. Take a deep breath. Let it go. There is only love and gratitude. "Yeah right," I hear some of you say. "I've had a crap day. Some idiot pulled out in front of me and I now have a scratch down the side of my car. The insurance ran out yesterday. It's going to cost me a fortune; which I don't have, and that holiday is out the window now... and you're telling me not to complain/criticise/blame?!"

Yes I actually am. I didn't say any of this flourishing malarky was easy. It's difficult to control your thoughts, rants and completely fair-enough complaints. But ranting about it won't change anything. You think it'll make you feel better, getting it off your chest. But it won't. The damage will still have been done to your car. You'll still have to fork out for that damage financially and sacrifice that well-earned holiday you'd been counting on. So you have a choice. You can be pissed off about it, tell every soul about how annoyed you are, cry, punch something and generally kick off, or you can take my advice. Take a ginormously deep breath. Say, "ok, this completely sucks, but I can't do anything about it. It wasn't my fault (if it was your fault, have a word with yourself to learn from that mistake) so I choose not to complain. I will give myself a well-deserved treat in a different way than a holiday in an under-£50-way to pat myself on the back for making that choice. Sh1t happens. Next? What am I grateful for? What went well today?" Rather than what went wrong today... by seizing control (which does take a LOT of practice) over your thoughts and feelings, you can improve your life. Annoying things will still happen but incredibly amazing things will too; and they will happen in ABUNDANCE - far more frequently than if you continued to rant and complain (in which case you'll attract more annoying stuff). If you focus your attention on the good stuff: on appreciating, on loving, on gratitude, you will attract more stuff to be grateful for, you'll feel good and attract more good. Good huh?

Remember – your thoughts and reactions create your reality. In the past we sewed the seeds of our future. Each word that we spoke, each thought that we held, each action that we took, created what is happening to us now and will happen to us in the future. When you realise that **your future depends on what you think about, what you say and what you do RIGHT NOW,** you'll want to think good thoughts, say good things and take positive action. Positive thinking really is a no-brainer.

Positive thinking can be even more powerful than positive action. Taking action obviously helps to make things happen. Being active instead of passive is no doubt the preferable way of being if you want to get what you want from life. And yet, it is often more about how we actively manage our thoughts and feelings that can have the most impact. Yep. While we just sit still, we can create more positive change, by doing nothing (and appearing passive) yet actively thinking the right way and feeling the right way, we can actively transform our life and attract all that we have ever wanted. Thinking is powerful. Feeling is powerful. That's why I say 'think unlimited'. Don't let limiting beliefs restrict you. If you take action because you don't really believe that your hearts desire will be delivered to you unless you do something, positive thinking may be tough. However, if you take action in an inspired way, moved and commanded by your solid and certain belief that your dreams will come to fruition, that's much easier and far more enjoyable.

In their resilience training course for soldiers, Sara Algoe and Barbara Fredrickson reveal that "it is through cultivating the positive that we are able to learn, grow and flourish." They explain: "You have the power within you to figure out what inspires you, what makes you laugh, or what gives you hope, and to cultivate those emotions... This can help you optimize your life by setting up moments of genuine positivity for yourself. These moments can help you to build your own resources that can be drawn upon. Moreover, the positive effects of your emotions can spread to other people." Spreading positivity and boosting morale as well as living it! Being positive just got a whole lot more wonderful because joyfulness is more contagious than sadness.

And don't worry, positive thinking isn't about replacing every single negative thought with a positive one. It's about pausing, considering and putting things into perspective. It's more about thinking critically rather than irrationally, so that you can stop the spiral of negative thoughts and evaluate the most likely scenario, rather than focusing on the worst-case scenario. Positive critical thinking is an enabling tool to help you be real, prevent unnecessary worrying and continue on an upward spiral rather than a downward one.

3. **Look on the BRIGHT SIDE.** Sadly, it is much easier to be grumpy than sustaining happiness which can take some effort. Us humans annoyingly have what's known as a "negativity bias." This means we focus on or react more strongly to negative comments, situations or events than we do positive comments, situations or events. According to research "it takes as least five good acts to repair the damage of one critical or destructive act." I remember reading Geri Halliwell's biography in which she admitted that, although switching on the Christmas Lights for the first

time in Oxford Street was an incredibly positive event for the Spice Girls, and one which filled them with elation and awe at the volume of people (the crowds screaming their names, the love and admiration and good vibes...) she will always remember the solitary person in the crowd who looked at her and shouted abuse.

My first book, *The Small Business Start-Up Workbook* has consistently sold well and stayed in the top 5 in the start-up category and top 25 in the small business category on Amazon since it was published in 2005. It has gained 29 amazingly positive glowing reviews. And yet, until I learned the power of flourishing, the one solitary negative review it received (which merely mentioned my over-use of exclamation marks and self-help focus on inspiration) upset me more, cast self-doubt and niggled me than any of the positive reviews had buoyed me. It affected me more than the sum of the rest of the brilliant reviews did. Sad but true. So what can be done? I now realise that 29 people have taken the time to recommend my book and write incredibly kind words of support. My book has helped them. The one person who wrote a negative review is right, there are too many exclamation marks (it was my first book) although I disagree with some of his other comments. But he is just one person, so I am very lucky to only have one poor review, given that we have by default a negativity bias and focus on the negative. Because, given that fact, we are more likely to bother spending time writing reviews if they are poor ones. We are a critical species. We only write positive reviews if we are really blown away; super impressed. So, yay! I'm glad the majority of people liked my book.

- **Put up a positivity shield.** Those who do enjoy positive emotion on a regular basis have a gremlin to face – other peoples' bad moods. Moods are contagious. If someone is feeling anxious, fed up, mistreated or miserable they will often flag up their bad mood and invite you to join their misery-guts party, but will also put a damper on your good fortune or happy moments. They might tell an excited you that you're wasting your time submitting your manuscript to publishers; they might suggest that your investing in a workshop on marketing is a waste of money because of the recession. The trick is to prevent these gremlins from curbing your enthusiasm and instead remain upbeat. Don't let other people's misery grind you down. If someone you love is having a hard time, do what you can - advise them, console them, reassure them, point them in the right direction so they can take action to resolve whatever is bothering them; then, once all is being done to rectify things or to make them feel better, try to get them to focus on the bright side (see below). If the gremlin is not a loved one, put up a shield and back away from them. Don't let them pollute your mood with their toxic negativity.

- **Take the rough with the smooth.** Accept that there will be things you don't like about people, situations, work, life... When you start a relationship/friendship with someone, take on a job or task, embrace that there is a whole package, part of which may not be as likeable as the rest. Some of that package will be what attracted you to that person/job/situation in the first place and some of it will bother you. It's just the way life is. You can either grumble about the bits that bother you or focus on the bits that you like and enjoy. Only one of these will make you happy. *The Rules of Life* author Richard Templar puts it best when he says: *"Life is a pizza. The best things in life come with chewy dried tomatoes and olives. There's no point moaning. Just pick them off, or swallow them down as fast as you can, and then sink your teeth into what's left and relish every bite."*

- **Shine a light on the upside; the good stuff.** If it rained on holiday for the first two days or you had a terrible cold in the run up to Christmas, say, "well at least it didn't rain for the entire time" and "at least I was completely well for the main event." By making a proper effort to look on the bright side of life, to see that upside in every negative situation, to see the positive traits among the negative characteristics in every person, to search for it and grasp it tightly - that is a worthy talent to practice. It keeps you sailing through rough seas. See crises as adventures; see flaws as interesting characteristics.

EXERCISE:

Spend this week talking only about the positive bright side of things. Do not complain, moan, whinge, not even once. Really be mindful of this. Note down any time you complain. Try harder next week.

- **Block negative thinking** by spending a minute affirming good stuff every time a negative limiting belief or resentful thought pops into your mind. Say 'I'm willing to see this in a different light. Let's give it a try' and then affirm some good stuff, take a deep breath and distract yourself from those negative thoughts. Create better thoughts and move on. If you cannot shift those negative thoughts and spiral towards an irrational pit of doom, consider why this might be? What can you learn from this negative thought pattern? Also use this time to pause, evaluate and think critically if you are unable to think positively. Have a word with yourself. You are going to be all right no matter what.

- **Think Unlimited!** Don't conspire with limiting beliefs or situations or conditions. They will hold you back. And don't just wait for conditions to change either – open your mind and become aligned with the realms of possibility and flourish.

- **Breathe love in and out.** To stop negative thoughts in their tracks and embrace peacefulness try this breathing exercise. Breathe in deeply and focus on feeling love for all that you can possibly love – your mister or missus, your family, your children, your pets, the wider world, just focus on feeling love in your heart as you breathe in, and then as you breathe out. Repeat ten times and you will open your eyes feeling way more positive than when you closed them.

- **Distract yourself from rumination and direct your thinking onto a better path.** Idle minds tend to dwell. We ruminate on events that have made us sad; on unreasonable, unpleasant or unfair situations. This rumination creates negative emotion. Women in particular tend to ruminate while men will tend to distract themselves.

  If you find yourself ruminating and/or worrying/having negative thoughts, you can either

  a) take decisive action and DO something to take your mind off that negative thought path. Or
  b) you can distract and interrupt your thought process by creating what Gretchen Rubin, author of *The Happiness Project*, calls "a mental area of refuge" This is a place you take your mind to as soon as a negative or brooding thought breaks through your positivity. It's a place where you think about lovely things which make you smile and feel instantly more positive again. For example, I think about my daughter laughing as we walk to school or being tickled as she runs happily on the beach, and so on. You might also revisit funny moments that made you laugh or make up a silly poem in your head.

  The key is to distract yourself from brooding by interrupting that negative thought-pattern and distracting yourself via thoughts/actions/memories to ultimately shift your thinking from negative to positive before moving on and carrying on with your day. Brain scans have shown that when you interrupt your thought-process with a happy thought (by visiting your 'mental area of refuge) blood surges into the left pre frontal cortex which refuels positivity and feelings of happiness. Hooray!

- **Be optimistic.** Studies show that optimism is a major contributor to growth, resilience and psychological fitness. Furthermore, mastery and optimism can strengthen the body in terms of health whereas helplessness and pessimism can weaken health. Researchers have found that optimism protects while pessimism hurts. Optimists bounce back, achieve more and even live longer, according to research which revealed that optimists are less likely to develop or die from certain illnesses. So, see setbacks as temporary rather than permanent and see victories as long-lasting. Know that YOU are in control. Expect good results. And, if you don't get good results, if you don't get what you want, know that the plan for your life far exceeds the circumstances of today. You've succeeded in the past and will do so again. Everyone, even the most optimistic, have days which don't go to plan. And so the only way is up and we carry on and try again or shift course and try something new.

It is even more important to try to be optimistic if you are a mother because, when studying why some people are more optimistic than others, Martin Seligman, author of *Learned Optimism: How to Change Your Mind and Your Life* says that "There's a markedly high correlation between your level of optimism and your mother's." So, if you want your child to gain the benefits that optimists have, be one yourself. If it doesn't come naturally, practice. Apart from hereditary conditioning, pessimists are often the way they are as a consequence of failing repeatedly at something or being fed limiting beliefs and thus they come to expect failure, to expect the worst rather than the best. This can take time to crack but it is possible.

How? By using the tools, actions and strategies in this very book. By smiling more; by having a debate with your negative thoughts to respond in a more positive way; by stopping blaming yourself and by considering why you are glad to be you rather than someone worse off than you; by focusing on fond memories and distracting yourself from pessimistic thoughts; by doing an activity that will lift you whenever you feel yourself slipping; by exercising, walking, breathing mindfully. As you turn the pages of this book you will become more and more equipped to learn and practice optimism and become more of an optimist. You always have a choice. Choose optimism.

- **Believe that your goodness will be rewarded**. It truly will. Sometimes it seems that you are putting in so much effort and can see other people who seemingly don't work as hard as you do being rewarded. Or perhaps you go out of your way to be generous and kind while people are rude and mean to you. Please don't lose faith in humanity or karma or the law of attraction (or whatever you want to call it). Goodness and effort begets reward and it's important to keep on putting in the effort and being decent because at some point you will be rewarded. It's so important to BELIEVE that; to *know* that good things WILL come. You might see it then as being lucky, but it's a belated reward for the good efforts. If you remain **positive, patient and persistent,** you will achieve what you believe in. To paraphrase Napoleon Hill "Conceive, believe, work hard and achieve." Instead of constantly seeking the reward, try to forget about it. Just know that it will come and remove the need to be rewarded from your mindset. Know. Believe. And keep on keeping on.

There is a trick at work here though. We don't always get what we want and sometimes, even if we've been positive and grateful and kind and cheerful, bad stuff can still happen. These two things can then destroy our belief that we will get what we want, that all shall be well and disappointment replaces gratitude, resentment replaces love, bitterness replaces appreciation and so we create the negative loop and attract more bad stuff and our thoughts self-fulfil. Instead, when we don't get what we want, there will be a reason for that – it could be that the job, house, relationship we were desperate to get wasn't actually right for us and didn't fit with our dream. It may not have been good enough for you to fit with your true desire and destination. Something more worthwhile is on its way and you need to believe that in order to manifest it. Often times the best things in our life appear just as we are about to throw in the towel and give up, just as we are about to stop believing. The bad stuff is there to test us, to strengthen us, to prepare us, to make us appreciate the good stuff when it happens. Just. Believe.

- **Be decent**. Do the right thing. This generally boils down to being trustworthy, honest, reliable and loyal. It means being thoughtful, helpful, considerate and friendly.

- **Worry less**. Worrying does not change the thing you're worrying about, except, according to the Law of Attraction, making it *more* likely to happen. According to Martin and Marion Shirran and Fiona Graham, "a thought can only take up as much space in your head as you allow it to." If you say that to yourself a few times you can prevent worrying thoughts from taking over your mind-space and choose to think about something else. Petty problems don't bother people who've been through proper tragic stuff. Even bigger problems can be dealt with.

The fact is: you never know what tomorrow will bring. You could devote a wholeentire day to worrying about something only for tomorrow to bring amazing news. You'll wish you hadn't wasted yesterday worrying about something you had no control over, because you can't get that time back. We've all done that. And yet *Que Sera Sera* – Whatever will be, will be.

If you are worrying about something that you DO have an element of control over then stop worrying and DO something about it. If it's about money, look into ways to reduce your outgoings and boost your incomings, set a budget. If a health issue is troubling you, go and see your doctor. If you are worried about a friend, talk to her or your mutual friends or get information that might help. If you are worrying about something that there is no solution for, that you can do nothing about... just stop worrying.

And remember this. Often, in life, when we look back at events with hindsight, it is those disastrous moments that seemed terrible at the time, which we can sometimes laugh at and, as such, create the best memories.

- **Wash it all away.** Karen Salmansohn calls this a "shower power meditation." It involves focusing on the feeling of water on you, washing away negative thoughts and actually visualising those negative thoughts of anger, fear, guilt and regret swirling down the plug hole. See ya!

4. **Bring your own sunshine and embrace your emotions.** We are born smiling. Indeed, smiling is one of the most basic biological uniform expressions of all humankind. And yet, as we leave childhood we smile less. While a third of us smile more than 20 times a day and laugh around 17 times daily,

children smile as many as 400 times a day, the same number of times that they laugh.

Oh to be a child again.

Thankfully we can still harness the power of smiling, regardless of age. Yes smiling is a very powerful thing. It's even more powerful than chocolate and money. As Ron Gutman revealed in a 2011 talk on TED, "Smiling stimulates our brain reward mechanism in a way that even chocolate, a well regarded pleasure-inducer, cannot match. British researchers found that just one smile can generate the same level of brain stimulation as 2000 bars of chocolate or receiving £16,000 in cash!"

> *"Even the simulation of an emotion tends*
> *to arouse it in our minds,"*
> Charles Darwin, 1872

Evidently, smiling, laughing, hugging and even crying are scientifically good for us. Yes, having a good sense of humour makes good sense.

> *"I will never understand what a simple*
> *smile can accomplish,"*
> Mother Theresa.

- **Smile more.** Even if you don't feel like smiling, fake it. According to research, happier emotions can be induced even from an artificial smile. You could even create a little routine every time you drink a glass of water or go to the toilet, you could sit there and smile. Nobody can see you. Try it. See what happens. How much you smile while you chat to someone is linked directly to their perception of your friendliness as well as your level of confidence. The act of smiling makes us feel better, whether or not we feel the emotion behind the smile. Furthermore, it's not only good for our well-being, it's great for our health too. Smiling can help reduce stress enhancing hormones like cortisol, adrenaline and dopamine and increase the level of mood-enhancing hormones such as endorphins, whilst also reducing blood pressure.

Smiling also has the power to brighten up other people's days and boost how positively others see you. A Swedish study found recently that it's difficult to frown when looking at someone who is smiling which makes smiling rather contagious, just like laughter. Sometimes just hearing someone else laugh will cause even the stoniest face to crack a smile. And when you do so, you appear more likeable, courteous and confident to others.

Today then (and ideally all week from now on) embrace your face and bring your emotions to the forefront. Be sunny.

- **Laugh more.** LOL! Children have an immensely humorous attitude. Sometimes we berate our children for messing about or being silly, when they are simply embracing that humorous attitude and doing something that makes them laugh. Sure, discipline is important, but sometimes it can be freeing to go with the flow and laugh with them, even if it means you have to sing a song involving the words 'mummy is a silly poo'. Go with it from time to time.

  Laughter is more than just a pleasurable activity. Just like smiling, laughter has the power to boost immunity and lower blood pressure and cortisol levels. Laughter reduces anxiety and squishes stress. It increases people's tolerance for pain too AND 10 minutes of laughing is the equivalent of 20 minutes worth of aerobic exercise on the rower. High five laughter! There are activities such as Laughter Yoga and workshops to help you to laugh more available throughout the country. For example http://laughterpilot.co.uk/

Laughter is a source of social bonding, and it helps to reduce conflicts and diffuse tricky situations within relationships – at work, in marriage, among strangers. When people laugh together, they tend to talk and touch more and to make eye contact more frequently. I often use humour as a distraction when trying to nip my four-year-old-daughter's whining in the bud. It works.

Schedule in some laughter. No, seriously. This could involve a trip to a comedy club/renting or buying a funny DVD, watching the Comedy Channel, booking a girls night in/out, having a 'silly morning' with your children. (One of the benefits of working from home is that I can step away from my desk and watch a bit of telly while eating my lunch. It's the only time I watch TV, except weekend evenings). Rather than watch an Australian Soap or the tail end of *Loose Women* I now tune in to the Comedy Channel for reruns of *Friends*. Adding a little laughter to my lunchtime always perks me up.

WHAT/WHO MAKES YOU LAUGH?

Who makes you laugh most? List friends, family, radio show presenters? When do you recall laughing the most in recent times? Who made you laugh recently?

- **Hug more**. Hugging reduces and relieves stress by releasing oxytocin. Fact! One study which required participants to hug as many different people each day as they could over the course of the month, ideally five hugs per day (without getting into trouble) became happier.

- **Cry when you feel like it.** Don't stifle it. Embrace your tears. Crying is important. It releases pent up emotion. Suicides in men are three times higher than that of women, despite the fact that women often feel more depressed than men; maybe the way we express our emotions helps women to manage anger and frustrations in a more effective way? Clearly big boys *should* cry. Crying enables us to diffuse stress and ultimately stress less as a result of shedding some tears. Some scientists even believe that crying removes toxins, particularly stress hormones, from our blood stream. It is certainly calming and cathartic to have a good cry. This is due to the act of crying activating our sympathetic nervous system and the sedating parasympathetic nervous system. So, if you feel the need, let go and sob. It'll make you feel better.

FLOURISH PLANNER (ongoing)

Schedule in:
- Reminisce time – time once a week/fortnight/month to revisit happy memories.
- Laughter. (Make time to laugh. Schedule in a regular TV/DVD/ Book/Cinema/Night in or out/Trip to a comedy club).

Printable Quotes... to cut out n stick up

"The past is behind,

LEARN from it.

The future is ahead,

PREPARE for it.

The present is here,

LIVE it."

Thomas S Monson

"The energy of the mind is

the essence of life."

Aristotle

"Optimism is the faith that leads to achievement. Nothing can be done without hope and confidence,"

Helen Keller

"Nobody can go back and start a new beginning, but anyone can start today and make a new ending."

Maria Robinson

Part 2

Meaning, Purpose & Engagement

Chapter 4

MONTH FOUR: Create a Meaningful Life/ Career/Business with Purpose

Purpose Provides Essential Guidance, Growth and Pride

"The secret of happiness is having something meaningful to do, seeking purpose,"
John Burroughs

So why does a meaningful and purposeful life make for a happier one?

Well, studies reveal that optimism is easier to cultivate and obstacles easier to rise above if you are committed to a set of values, a cause, a purpose. Having a purpose strengthens your resolve to persist during tough times; it fills you with determination and bolsters your confidence. It's far easier to have the courage of your convictions if those convictions are woven into an overarching purpose.

By having a purpose and direction to guide us, we are more able to stretch ourselves, to do what it takes to fulfil our purpose, to rise to challenges we meet along the way. That purpose spurs and cheers us on. Furthermore, in having this purposeful agenda and meaningful aim we grow and, in growing, we flourish. As Oswald Spengler, German Philosopher (1880-1936) suggests: *"This is our purpose: to make as meaningful as possible this life that has been bestowed upon us; to live in such a way that we may be proud of ourselves; to act in such a way that some part of us lives on."*

"Challenges are what make life interesting;
overcoming them is what makes life meaningful,"
Joshua J. Marine

Furthermore, when we find a way to link our experiences into a meaningful pattern, we feel more *in control* of our life. We are consequently happier with our lot because we know what we're here for as each goal and action we take towards them are in harmony with each other; they make sense and create meaning. Conversely when life feels random and aimless, we feel more out of control and, studies show, less happy. Our life makes less sense and we care less about unfulfilled desires or expectations.

Flourishing from purpose is thus two-fold. On the one hand, if we feel that we are doing something with our lives which has a purpose, this gives our lives meaning and thus value (and control) which boosts our well-being. Secondly, if we have a purpose, we have a direction and therefore a place in which to flourish and grow. Growth and development are a powerful part of our overall well-being. If we feel that we are stuck, stagnant and failing to grow, this can have the knock-on effect of making us feel worthless, unfulfilled and pessimistic. Conversely, if we are striving for and working towards something, regardless of whether or not we are achieving that something, we are more likely to feel fulfilled and thus pleased with ourselves. This ties in with the final pillar of well-being: accomplishment and achievement. But more on that later.

Certainly working and living for a greater purpose is something that humans have a yearning for, and is the reason that we feel good about ourselves when we live a purposeful life. What's more, if we're in our element, i.e. if we're putting our talents to use to work on something that we're passionate about, that's when we feel most at ease, most authentic, most at home.

"Everything in the universe has a purpose. Indeed,
the invisible intelligence that flows through everything in
a purposeful fashion is also flowing through you."
Wayne Dyer

So having a compelling purpose gives our life essential meaning. Regardless of what our ultimate goal is, if our purpose enables us to become immersed in a series of actions towards clear objectives, it will bring significant meaning and order to our life and enable us to achieve unified optimal experience (we'll be looking at optimal experience and 'flow' in the following chapter). As such, everything we do then takes on this sense of directionality and enables us to have a clarity of vision and ability to enjoy our life's journey. We are better able to enjoy the journey when our life has meaning and purpose because we have come to terms with ourselves and our lives and we therefore know that, whatever is happening to us, it's all worthwhile. This gives us inner strength, serenity and bolsters our resolve to continue along the route we are on. That's a huge dose of well-being right there which helps us to thoroughly enjoy our experiences along the way.

"The meaning of life is meaning: whatever
it is, wherever it comes from,
a unified purpose is what gives meaning to life,"
Mihaly Csikszentmihalyi

Ultimately then, a unified purpose justifies our daily actions and spurs us on towards actualising our potential. The result is a more enjoyable life. Conversely, not doing what we love and are compelled to do in the wider sense can generate tension and a feeling of lacking.

A Sense of Values and Belonging

A meaningful life with purpose can also be a life where you feel that you belong to something which serves more than your self. This doesn't have to be some huge cause or religion or political party, although they are all valid. It could be that your purpose is to provide for your family or to create and support a community group; it could be a movement, such as The Guide Association. It could be a way of life, such as being ethical and green; kind to the environment, saving the planet. Having meaning and purpose in your life is feeling connected to something greater. This can apply to how you live your life in general and/or your working life.

If your job doesn't give you a sense of purpose but you enjoy it, you could try volunteering to bring an element of purpose into your life or focus on a wider purpose of kindness to create meaning in your life. Simply committing to spend more time with your family can give you a better sense of purpose. A family life that is filled with rich and meaningful family-focused experiences where your purpose is to be a good parent, to create a positive family experience and bring up your children to be good citizens and kind human beings with strong values – that is meaningful enough.

And therein lies another element of purpose – having strong values. Our values are shaped by what matters to us the most.

Only when you know yourself can you *be* yourself. So, about that...

Define Your Purpose: Shining A Torch on Your Life's Work

1. **Identify and define your core purpose, mission statement and values in life and work.** These will shape your actions and staying true to them will enable you to flourish in whatever you choose to do.

   - **Consider and answer these questions:**

     - **CAUSES: What matters most to you?** What core causes do you care about? What makes you cross? If you had a magic wand - what would you change in society? The glass ceiling? Fat cat bosses? Injustices? Unrealised potential? Poverty? War? Gender stereotyping? List what matters to you most:

_____

_____

_____

_____

_____

- **PASSION/SKILLS: What are your passionate about and what are you good at?** What activities do you love to do and experience? Writing? Being your own boss? Being with children? Inspiring others? Consider too what comes easily to you? What are you best at? (This could be the same as what you're passionate about) Writing? Teaching? Creating? Inspiring? Leading? Communicating?

_____

_____

_____

_____

_____

Using your **talents** and **passion** to **enable change** is the epitome of **motivation towards your purpose** – its the highest point where optimum ability meets optimum motivation and thus creates optimum fulfilment and success in pursuing a purpose. This may not have anything to do with what you do for a living. Finding your forte/element could mean pursuing what you are passionate about as a hobby or side project. It's about finding the right balance so that you can give your life more meaning.

- **VALUES: What do you/will you teach your children? What values do you want the way in which you live your life to reflect?** Good manners, cleanliness, kindness, positivity, family values, ambition, success, the environment, human rights, education?

_____

_____

_____

_____

_____

Does your life reflect these values? Sometimes, with so much going on, it can be really easy to lose sight of our core values, unless we have ingrained them into our own identity, in which case they provide a guiding light and the foundations on which our purpose is built.

How do you wish to be remembered? What do you hope to be your biggest accomplishments? To have inspired others? Provided a good life and stable foundations for your family? Published a book? Done things YOUR way? Left a legacy? To have got your children to adulthood "without breaking them (or yourself)" as a friend once commented?

_____

_____

_____

_____

_____

In his book, _The Seven Habits of Highly Effective People_, the late Stephen Covey said:

"Begin with the end in mind. Do my actions flow from my mission? What would you like the epitaph on your tombstone to read? Answering this should reveal exactly what matters most to you in your life. Create a personal mission statement [from this] to ensure that you are always working toward your most meaningful life goals."

What do you want to devote your time to? What deserves your attention? What is your mission in life going to be? For example, through my books thus far, through my business: WiBBLE, and through _The Flourish Handbook_ /Weekender and another project I have in the pipeline (and in my role as 'mum')

My purpose and mission statement is :

To inspire, inform, empower and enable others

Everything that I do, every action that I take, every business I establish, every blog post I write, every lesson

I try to teach my daughter... all of that is led and guided by that core purpose. Through this core purpose I aim to empower others to believe in themselves, enjoy their lives more, and reach their potential. My wider mission which ties in with this purpose is to gain more financial help for self-employed mums and put a stop to gender stereotyping (causes which I feel strongly about and am using my passion and skills to work on.)

MY PURPOSE: MY MISSION STATEMENT

What's yours? Write your own personal purpose/mission statement here:

My purpose and mission statement is:

_____

_____

_____

_____

_____

---

2. **Assess your work: does it provide you with a sense of purpose?** In carrying out your role, do you feel connected to a wider purpose/mission? For example, my first job after graduating was as Editorial Assistant for *Guiding/ Brownie* magazine. I loved that job, partly because it was my first step towards my ambition of becoming a writer and secondly because I felt part of something. I didn't realise it at the time but that job was my first role (not including being House Captain at school) which was part of a purpose to inspire, inform and empower, in this case, girls. The materials I worked on were guided by that purpose.

What else does your work provide you with? Recognition? Fun? Self-esteem? Social connection? An "atmosphere of growth?" If it doesn't provide you with these, which areas need the most attention? Perhaps you have lots of fun at work and your job provides you with a great sense of purpose and social connection, but perhaps there is limited scope for growth and a lack of recognition or reward. If so, come up with a plan of action to talk with your boss to praise what you love about the job and see if you could be motivated to stick around by having something to work towards and be recognised/rewarded for. If your job provides you with no real sense of purpose and doesn't tick many of these boxes, it could be time to rethink what you spend the majority of your life doing. It really is possible to look forward to Monday mornings as much as you relish the onset of Friday afternoon. (When you do so, make sure you are grateful for that.)

My work/job provides me with: _____

My work/job doesn't provide me with: _____

What I'm going to do about that is: _____

- **What business ideas or jobs do you feel passionate about?** Passion is a vital determinant in work related success. You need to feel enthusiastic about something in order to put in the required effort to make it work. You need to practice, work hard and stay determined even when the going gets tough, and this is far easier and less challenging to do if you absolutely LOVE what you do. What comes easily to you? What do you love to do professionally in the realm of work? What are you an expert in? What would you like to become an expert in? What makes you feel right/good? What makes you feel wrong/bad? Get scribbling:

Work-wise, I love to_____
These are my favourite tasks. Doing this makes me feel right/good.

_____comes easily to me.

I could consider myself an expert at/in_____

I'd like to know more about/become an expert in___

_____.

I'd rather not_____as these tasks make me feel bad. Can I delegate these to someone who enjoys these tasks/is better at them?

"Do what you love. Love what you do."

- **Consider whether you have a vocation; a calling to work as something in particular.** For example, I felt compelled to write this book and do whatever I can to inspire women and young people to flourish. I feel a calling to positive education. Currently that is through words (written and spoken); but it may also evolve into empowering people through teaching. While I am an author/writer/business woman and mum rather than a teacher I am still working within my vocation as a writer fulfilling a purpose to inform and inspire, empower and educate others.

What's your calling/vocation?

_____

_____

Are you following it?

What could you do over the coming months to pursue your calling (or take a step towards pursuing it)?

_____

_____

- **Are you living up to your own expectations? Are you on course to reach your potential in your career?** If not, can you pinpoint why? What could be done about this? What's blocking your route? Or could it be that you are expecting too much of yourself right now? You may be more than capable of reaching your potential but the timing could be wrong. Perhaps you could create a different path but still reach your potential? Or maybe you don't believe in yourself enough (even though you are actually brilliant!) This is a common issue. Maybe you need to give yourself a break (you're only human, not superhuman) and stop putting unrealistic expectations on yourself. For example, you may have taken time out to have children and see that as a block to your route of fulfilling your potential but, you are fulfilling your potential as a mother (the most important job in the world) and you could take tiny steps, month by month, to realise your career potential again, gradually. You might take on some evening work, do some voluntary work to get back into things, come up with a business plan so that you can pursue your passions and purpose once more. If the latter is the case, there's heaps of support, encouragement and tools available through my social business platform and online support network for self-employed women, WiBBLE http://www.WiBBLE.us.

3. **Know you. Be you. Be lucid and true to you.** Be precisely unswervingly true to yourself by applying the notes you have written down above to yourself. By understanding what makes you tick, what motivates you to enjoy working;

what you feel strongly about; your value set; your purpose and mission, you carve out your sense of identity. All of this makes you YOU! Don't be what you are expected to be or even what you expect yourself to be (based on outside influences). Gretchen Rubin, author of *The Happiness Project*, worried about feeling "legitimate" and decided that working in law would make her *feel* legitimate. And yet, her true passion was writing. She loved to write. She's good at it. Years later, she pursued her true purpose and passion and became a writer. It paid off and made her happier. Grow naturally, in your inherent and instinctive direction.

Focus on what is important to YOU! Understand where you are headed, which direction you want to take, feel compelled to take, because of who you are, what you enjoy and how you wish to live your life. Imagine the 90 year old you reminiscing... what do you hope you'll be able to look back on with joy? 'I'm glad I did that, so grateful I chose that path,' rather than, 'I wish I'd done that, I wish I hadn't done that'. That's the important stuff. Focusing on that important stuff, on what is uniquely important to you, that and being decent so that you don't inflict pain or hurt on others, they are the things that count in life. I mean really counts. Being a good parent and child and husband/wife/sibling/friend – they are important. Treating others as you wish to be treated is important. Looking after yourself and others is important. Accumulating material things isn't so vital when you look at it that way. Watching TV, getting the latest gizmo, making sure you know all the gossip? Not so much. Sharing your life with someone, being loved, loving back, following your rightful most meaningful purposeful path in life. Staying true to you. That's what is important. Try not to lose sight of that. In doing so you won't sweat the small stuff; you won't get so caught up in the woes of having to repay a tax credit overpayment or burning the toast again or worrying what people think of you. None of that REALLY matters does it?

In her book, *The Happiness Project*, Gretchen Rubin says *"To be happy, I need to think about feeling good, feeling bad, and feeling right, in an atmosphere of growth."* By this she means that you need to focus on things that will enable positive emotions by boosting enthusiasm, joy, pleasure, gratitude and friendship while also removing whatever might enhance negative emotions by decreasing guilt, envy, anger, annoyance, shame, regret, boredom and so on. That's the good and bad feelings, but what about feeling right? That comes down to being an authentic version of yourself – doing what you are supposed to be doing, for real, not what is expected of you but what you feel right doing, what you are good at doing, what you enjoy doing.

Keeping it real!

Find Your Strengths & Harness Your Abilities

There's NOBODY QUITE LIKE YOU! Nobody is exactly the same (even if you have a twin). You are unique and therefore brilliant. So what's your handprint? What's the hallmark of your character? What are your key signature strengths?

Because identifying your strengths and putting them to good use more often is a key way to boost your well-being. Not only does this give your life more meaning as already discussed, it enables you to better engage with the activities you enter into and go into what is known in positive psychology as 'flow'. But more on flow in Chapter 5.

"When you engage in systematic, purposeful action,
using and stretching your abilities to the maximum,
you cannot help but feel positive and confident abut yourself."
Brian Tracy

A simple rule in life, work and business is to play to your strengths.

1. **Define what you're good at. Find your forte. Identify then deploy your signature strengths.** How would people describe you? What are you known best for? What are your strengths and aptitudes? List five of your main strengths of character and five of your skills (e.g. STRENGTHS: organised, creative, confident, proactive, reliable, logical ... and then SKILLS: writing, editing, presenting, networking, troubleshooting, etc). Are you a creative thinker? Are you an opportunity-spotter? Are you logical and reliable or sociable and witty? What do you want to be known for? What excites you? Do these contrast with your aptitudes? If so, tell people when you've spotted an opportunity or had a creative idea. Walk the talk and people will remember you as that 'young girl with the creative energy' or 'the fast-learner who always delivers before deadline'. Walk the talk and make more of YOU and how you brand YOURSELF and you'll shine like you did as a child! Being an authentic version of yourself, being in your element, being someone who spends their time flexing and playing their strengths is a sure-fire way to sky-rocket your well-being.

MY STRENGTHS AND SKILLS

Strengths:

Skills:

Circle the words that best describe your key strengths. Then list them in order. Take the VIA Signature Strengths Survey http://www.authentichappiness.sas.upenn.edu/aiesec/Register.aspx to carry out a test that will list your strengths in order. There are many questions and it does take around 10 minutes to complete, but bear with it as it is incredibly accurate and very useful.

Leadership, organisation, confidence, articulate, teamwork, loyalty, creativity, lateral thinking, critical thinking, originality, honesty, diligence, perseverance, hard worker, fast learner, fairness, curiosity, open-mindedness, social awareness, empathy, kindness, generosity, optimism, positivity, playfulness, sense of humour, caring, enthusiasm, energy, prudence, bravery, courage, modesty, humility, spirituality, gratitude, self-control.

See how your perception of your core strengths measures up to your VIA Signature Strengths Survey results.

"Enter every activity without giving mental recognition to the possibility of defeat. Concentrate on your strengths, instead of your weaknesses... on your powers, instead of your problems."
Paul J. Meyer

- **Visit** http://www.authentichappiness.sas.upenn.edu/ aiesec/Register.aspx **to complete your signature strengths test.** It does take up 10 minutes or so of your time but it's completely worth it. Its accuracy is amazing.

- **Schedule using your signature strengths into your planner.** Positive psychologists believe that you can boost your life-satisfaction if you identify and then use your signature strengths as frequently as you can at school, at home, during hobbies, as well as at work. For example, if creativity is one of your top 5 strengths, plan to spend some time writing an eBook or novel, creating a scrapbook or photo collage or designing some t-shirts or products. If kindness is one of your strengths, schedule in some acts of kindness. If self-control is one of your strengths, schedule in some time to plan a nutritious menu or do some exercise. Use your strength in new ways that you haven't tried before; try to challenge yourself. Consider how engaged in the activity you felt.

The more you utilise your core strengths the more likely you are to enjoy a good sense of well-being. There are all kinds of ways you can harness your skills in your work and your life. For example, those with creativity as a core strength might redesign a room in their home, audition for something, take an evening class in photography, pottery, painting, fine art, creative writing or feng shui; design and make your own birthday cards for friends and family; read biographies of famously creative people. If leadership is one of your core strengths, flex your leadership muscles by becoming a sports coach for a youth sporting team; organising a fundraising event within your local community, starting up a communal garden and getting support from your community, reading biographies of your favourite leaders and jotting down key points you've learned; mentoring someone.

- **List times when you have been useful to others.** Perhaps a friend asked you for advice, listened, took it and benefited as a direct result? Perhaps a work colleague or boss asked you to carry out a certain task and was suitably impressed by your input? In doing this exercise you may uncover strengths and abilities that you took for granted.

_____

_____

_____

_____

_____

- **Describe you at your best.** Do this as if you were trying to persuade an employer to hire you for your dream job.

  _____

  _____

  _____

  _____

  _____

- **Consider opportunities you have seized or missed.** Times where your strengths have been / could have been fully utilised. What would you do differently with the benefit of hindsight? When doors have closed, what doors have subsequently opened?

  _____

  _____

  _____

  _____

  _____

- **Consider strengths you have which you might inspire others with or pass on to others.** What can you pass on? Skills, talents, knowledge, passion... what you know/do/ feel about something can inspire a whole new generation of people or your own generation. What's the point in keeping everything to yourself? It's not possible to empty your brain and pass on EVERYTHING you have learned but you can give people advice and tips, share your story, tell people about the mistakes you've made, what you might do differently with the benefit of hindsight and about your best decisions, choices and successes and your worst decisions too. You may well think that you have nothing to give, nothing of value to share, but that would be unfair to say because you most definitely know stuff that I don't know and that others don't know. You know how to do things that other's don't. So pass it on. Passing things on will make you feel good.

When I set up WiBBLE I wanted to share my knowledge with other self-employed women in business. With my work purpose being to inspire, inform, empower and enable others, this seemed like the next natural step. Dumping knowledge I'd gleaned over the years into a variety of formats: eBooks, eCourses, Toolkits, Worksheets and so on, and setting up networking events and fayres where others could showcase their own skills, was the result. And it feels good. The same is true of this very handbook. If you learn just one new skill,new way of thinking, and implement even one change to the way you live your life and boost your well-being and/ or reach your potential as a result, that is worth every single minute that I've spent researching, writing and crafting this book. It's a worthwhile thing to share. So think about what skills, experience and knowledge you may be able to share with others.

Create a Purposeful Business with a Values-Led Ethos

You may find that playing to your strengths and putting your skills into practice to pursue your passion leads you towards being your own boss. Running your own business with a mission of it's own is one of the most meaningful and purposeful activities you can do. However, in order to flourish, your business should have strong values and an overarching purpose. Not only to make it easier to stay passionate when times are tough and obstacles need to be overcome, but because your business will stand out from the competition and feel right if it has a values-led ethos at its heart.

Frankly, today's consumers are increasingly immune to brands thanks to over-marketing and branding overload, which has desensitized people to brands and the messages they churn out. That's why, today, the best way to create affinity with your brand is to make sure it stands for something; to have a true purpose at the heart of your business. It is that which will capture peoples' hearts and minds and compel them to sit up and take notice, not your prices or your products' features, but your purpose that people can relate to, believe in and trust. The result is a business that people will buy into and stay loyal to; creating brand longevity.

Regardless of the size of your business, whether you are the founder of a large corporation or run a little cake-baking-business from home, your organisational values and what you stand for in the marketplace are more crucial than ever before. Purpose becomes the precursor for everything else - it influences actions and decisions, principles and values, culture and PR angles. An organisation's purpose and subsequent set of values should therefore be embedded into the very heart of the company. And, if you have no staff and, like me, run your business from the comfort of your home on your own, it is far easier to be passionate about your business if it has meaning; if it has a purpose. Standing for something, having a strong purpose and thus brand personality enables businesses to cultivate strong internal and external relationships and engage with each stakeholder in the business: customers, investors, staff, partners and suppliers.

1. **Define your business purpose and contribution.** You are much more likely to create a viral buzz around your brand if you have a clear purpose. The Body Shop famously turned their shops into action stations for human rights. "We

lobbied our customers to speak out on issues that affected them. It meant that we used spaces to create an atmosphere, deliver a message and make a point," the late great Dame Anita Roddick told me when I interviewed her for my *Small Business Start-Up Workbook*. It is this all-encompassing purpose that informs the mission of the company and it is that well-defined mission which dictates the overall strategy, growth plan, brand identity and vision of an organisation.

For example:

- The Body Shop's purpose is to support community trade, activate self-esteem, defend human and animal rights and protect the planet. The company even has its human rights purpose written into its Memorandum of Association. The majority of Body Shop customers and employees are people who relate to and/or share those values with the company they buy from/work for.
- Google's purpose is to organise the world's information and make it universally accessible and useful.
- Avon's purpose, according to its CEO, Andrea Jung, is to "empower women one woman at a time to learn how to earn."
- Feel Good Drinks' purpose is to "create a product that puts a smile on people's faces."
- Apple's purpose is to innovate, to create a positive user experience and design aesthetically pleasing products.
- Skype's purpose is to taken on the Telcos by providing an alternative via low cost and free calls over the Internet.

And, more generally:

- Street sweepers' purpose is to make the locality a nicer and cleaner place to live and work.
- Car hire companies and taxi firms purpose is to make peoples' daily lives less stressful.

What contribution will you make to people's lives? Therein lies the core of your branding. And if you can zoom in on a market or story that people are keen to talk about and create a buzz, even better.

- What's your business's purpose?

  e.g. WiBBLE's is to inspire, inform, empower and enable self-employed women to believe in themselves, find more time, get more focused, get more customers and create a successful business.

- What contribution will you make to peoples' lives?

  We provide _____ with _____

  _____ so that they can

  _____

e.g. We provide self-employed women with tools, knowledge and learning materials (worksheets, planners, tutorials, eCourses, checklists) along with support, a community of like-minded women and a promotional platform so that they can boost their self-confidence, achieve their goals, solve their problems, and succeed in business by selling more stuff.

- What point do you want to make? What message do you want to get across?

  e.g. WiBBLE wants to prove that anyone can do it, that being self-employed enables mums to be more flexible and provides a worthwhile opportunity to make money and follow a passion. WiBBLE is also on a mission to get better financial support for self-employed home-run business owners.

_____

_____

_____

_____

- What personality do you want to put out there?

_____

_____

_____

_____

e.g. the WiBBLE brand personality needed to be bold and bright and 'inspired by Wonder Woman' and thus be strong, vibrant, bold and dynamic. The brand identity (logo, colours, website and other collateral) capture that personality.

- What do you want to do better than anyone else? And, in doing so, play to your strengths?

e.g. in contrast to other membership sites, WiBBLE provides practical tools, solutions and support that are valuable yet uniquely affordable (ranging from £7 to £47).

_____

_____

_____

_____

2. **Define your values; your set of ideals, attitudes, methods of doing things.** Your values enable people to see how you, as a business, rank the importance of certain things. Your business will then be positioned in their mind according to those values and, in turn, you'll attract a following of customers who relate to and concur with those values.

In fact, these purpose-led values can be so powerful that they make your business a "come-to" brand. i.e. the *only* logical choice when people want a certain product. So, if people want a certain widget they come to this company for it, not just because they make widgets, but because they are the widget company which stands out from the rest because they have a powerful set of brand values and a strong and clearly articulated purpose.

In order to become a 'come to brand' businesses should:

- Focus on their strengths, on what they are really good at.
- Focus on their purpose and values, on what they stand for.
- Shout about those strengths and that purpose from the rooftops. Package up the brand and then articulate and communicate it clearly.

For instance:
- Apple clearly ranks style over price sensitivity. Their values of innovation, style and creativity make the brand synonymous with those values. This makes them a 'come to' business. If people want innovative, stylish products they 'come to' Apple.
- If people want high quality audio and televisual solutions they 'come to' Bang & Olufsen.
- If people want cheap and cheerful solutions they 'come to' easyGroup.

- If people want high quality services for people 50 and over, they go to Saga.
- If women business owners want uniquely affordable yet valuable business tools and support, they go to WiBBLE.

What are your brand values?

If people want_____

they come to [insert your business name]_____

3. **Generate a PR buzz by focusing in on your purpose.** By packaging up your purpose, articulating and communicating it, you'll be able to build a strong relationship with the consumer, get your message across to a clearly defined audience with more clarity and create a brand that people want to talk about. Companies pay millions to achieve that and many fail.

   - **Find a purposeful and timely PR angle** What publications (online and offline) do your target audience read? Inside those publications what themes are recurrent? For example, are there a wealth of stories about how to live your life more positively or healthily or more environmentally-friendly? If you can present journalists who write for these publications and blogs, with a product which plays into that story or theme, it's a no-brainer for them to write about it.

     My target audience reads the following magazines, blogs:

     _____

     _____

     _____

     _____

Recent themes over the past three – six months have included:

_____

_____

_____

_____

My business brand ties in well with these themes because:

_____

_____

_____

_____

4. **Create a purposeful brand identity** which captures your ethos, purpose and personality.

   - **Design a logo that captures your purpose and personality**, which highlights the company's heritage or emphasizes your environmental stewardship and core values.
   - **Brainstorm characteristic keywords that your brand should evoke** (e.g. fun, stylish, warm, bold, efficient).
   - **List keywords that evoke feelings, visual imagery or action-based memories** that your brand should communicate (eg Christmas holidays, family Sunday roast, falling in love, feeling free, strolling along the beach, keeping fit and feeling strong & healthy). These will make your brand really mean something.
   - **Assess your brand name.** The best names tend to share common characteristics – they infuse purpose and

personality into the name, often have few syllables, are phonetic and easy to remember.

- **Check that the brand names on your shortlist are available as web addresses.** Making sure that your domain name is available and not already taken is vital.
- **Present your brand persona consistently.** Create a branding template and style guide detailing font faces and sizes along with print and web colour values.

To Do List and Planner

Identify & define my PURPOSE/MISSION/VALUES in Life/work/biz !

Asses my work & vocation. Devise actions to take.

Identify my ☺ Signature strengths

FLOURISH PLANNER (ongoing)

Schedule in:

1. Deployment of signature strengths into social, work, family life/activities
2. Actions based on assessment of work/career/biz.
3. Actions to pursue your calling/vocation.

Printable Quotes... to cut out n stick up

"The only way to do great work is to love what you do. If you haven't found it yet, keep looking. Don't settle."

Steve Jobs

"Passion is energy. Feel the power that comes from focusing on what excites you."

Oprah Winfrey

"It's never too late to be

what you might have been,"

George Eliot

"It's never too late to be

what you might have been,"

George Eliot

Chapter 5

MONTH FIVE: Sourcing Engagement and Enjoyment

*"Unless a person takes charge of them,
both work and free time are likely to be disappointing,"*
Mihaly Csikszentmihalyi, Author of *Flow*

How to Enjoy Your Life More & Optimise The Quality of Your Experiences

So far we've covered a whole range of topics from tackling your environment and your mind to earning from (and letting go of) the past. In the next few chapters we'll focus our attention on the balance between making the most of right **now** and equipping yourself for a brighter **future**.

In this chapter we'll explore the notion of 'flow' and 'engagement' regarding what you choose to spend your time doing and, more importantly, *how* you do it in terms of optimising your enjoyment of each and every experience that you have right now.

By optimising each experience we live, NOW becomes instantly more enjoyable. How wonderful is that?

You see, to improve your life and boost your well-being, you must improve the quality of experience. Instilling this quality control over your day-to-day experiences will enable you to enjoy your journey through life far more.

This is contrary to popular belief that, to improve your life you must gain symbols of happiness (such as wealth and status). That awesome car, impressive home and slender body won't automatically give you happiness and improve your life. Struggling endlessly to reach these goals is the status quo. It's just what we do. Yet, while living in your dream home with your dream body, your dream partner and your dream car on the driveway may make you feel better and give you a good sense of well-being, that feeling is not sustainable due to the in-built human hedonic treadmill of constantly wanting more once each goal is achieved. So, while these goals are still worth striving for, (see Chapter 8 about goal setting, achievement and enjoying the journey) they are only part of the jigsaw puzzle of an enjoyable life and a satisfied self.

Another crucial part of this jigsaw is not reachable through the pursuit of such goals, it is only achieved by improving the quality of experience within your day-to-day life. Right here, right now, as they happen. By enabling more flow and engagement into our lives TODAY, we can build a better TOMORROW.

Optimising experience and flow is about mastery, participation and control. In choosing the content of your life (the activities and goals you pursue and how you pursue them) you are empowered to enjoy your life more through the choices that you make.

In order to control the level of quality of our experiences we need to choose activities that we know we can enjoy and feel most engaged in on a daily basis.

There are three core objectives that achieve this.

1. **GET IMMERSED TO OPTIMISE EXPERIENCE**: To become so absorbed, involved and engaged in what you do through the level of concentration and attention that you pay activities, that you enter a state of sustained involvement or 'flow', otherwise known as 'optimal experience'.

2. **GROW WITH THE FLOW TO EXPAND YOURSELF:** To stretch yourself and your skills when you do stuff by setting the right level of challenge and clear goals to strive for, so that you may improve those skills and subsequently grow.
3. **CHOOSE ABSORBING ACTIVITIES TO BOOST ENJOYMENT AND GRATIFICATION:** To do more of what you love and less of what you don't so that you can thoroughly enjoy your experiences.

All of these equate to being more 'autotelic'; more in control of your life and how you live it. And, in being so, you become empowered so that even the smallest experiences can create deep joy and satisfaction; whether it's smelling baking bread as you stroll past a bakery or enjoying the feeling of a cool and crisp breeze on a stifling hot day; or perhaps watching your child play imaginatively with her toys; moving a business proposition to the next stage; noticing the first signs of spring as a daffodil sways lightly in the wind...

Ultimately, achieving flow in your daily life and ticking the above trio of boxes enables you to improve your immediate experiences and, consequently, ENJOY THE JOURNEY.

So let's tackle these requirements of optimal experience one-by-one, step-by-step.

Get Immersed To Optimise Experience

Cast your mind back over your life thus far and consider which have been the best moments, the most enjoyable and exhilarating experiences of your life? For example, I'd include giving birth to my daughter, abseiling for charity, receiving the first copy of my first book, meeting some of my idols, roller skating with friends. All of these moments were active. They involved either accomplishing something which stretched me to use my strengths or an achievement of a goal. Surprisingly they do not include any passive, chilled-out moments of pleasure. Whilst I cherish the moments when peace and quiet descends on my house, when everyone is fed, my daughter is snugly sleeping safe and sound upstairs, and I have the place to myself, the most memorable moments are notably active rather than passive; they are the result of activities that I completely immersed myself in. The passive moments of having the freedom to enjoy my own company and choose whatever I wish to do of an evening do fill me with deep joy; but I cannot count those moments as the best experiences of my life. It is those which took courage or persistence and utilised my strength and ambition which generated the most gratification. I had to *do* something in order to make them happen. Just as Mihaly Csikszentmihalyi, author of *Flow* says, "Optimal experience is something that we make happen."

So what precisely is flow? In short, it's a heightened level of engagement in what you are doing. I'll leave it to the man who coined the phrase to explain in more detail: "Flow," says Mihaly Csikszentmihalyi, "is the state in which people are so involved in an activity that nothing else seems to matter; the experience itself is so enjoyable that people will do it even at great cost, for the sheer sake of doing it."

In his book he outlines that there are certain criteria or 'phenomenology of enjoyment' that activities must have to enable this deeply optimally enjoyable flow. They are activities which:

- We have a chance of completing due to having appropriate/ adequate skills.
- We are able to concentrate on.
- We are able to exercise control over.
- Have clear goals and provide immediate feedback regarding how well we are doing.
- Enable us to lose self-consciousness.
- Enable us to forget about everyday worries.
- Cause time to stand still or be distorted, so that an hour feels like a matter of minutes or vice versa.

The joy and gratification that people gain from activities in which 'flow' is optimised means that they will do that activity regardless of cost or risk, regardless of what they gain from doing it, just because they love to do it and feel utterly absorbed in it.

Initially, you may think that this list of criteria fits only sporting activities or competitive games, such as tennis, dancing, football, climbing or chess; or artistic and creative endeavours which involve escaping from reality or making something — stuff that you can truly immerse yourself in. However, typically mundane tasks, such as queuing in line for a theatre show or mowing the lawn can be transformed from mundane to enjoyable by implementing these rules. For example, you could focus your attention on mowing the lawn, set yourself a time limit within which to mow a certain area and consider each daisy head chopped off or avoided as a point scored. The act of mowing the lawn then becomes automatic (and thus more enjoyable) as you focus your concentration on the goals you have set and enter your own little world of lawn-mowing bliss.

Whether you are a dancer working seamlessly through moves in a routine or a mother enjoying the experience of reading to her daughter, you will be given feedback, either from the approving nod of a dance teacher or a feeling that you got that move exactly right, or from the silence of listening, warm smile or shared laughter between you and your child. If you are fully immersed in that activity and feel like you lose touch with the outside world, you are experiencing flow. Indeed, dancing or reading to your child are all that's on your mind — just that activity — nothing else. Once you're into it, you're into it and you're in control.

As you go about your daily life over the coming week, pay attention to those activities which enable you to lose touch with the outside world, no matter how momentarily. Explore your flow.

Flow though is not the normal status of affairs. Nope. The status quo is to continually interrupt our activities and thoughts with questions and concerns. 'Should I be doing this now? What about such and such?... I wonder how so and so is? I hope so and so isn't in a bad mood tonight.... Ooh I must remember to put the rubbish/dog/recycling out' and so on. This 'entropy' as it's known is our regular state of mind, where we automatically think about current problems, grudges or frustrations and give those thoughts precedence. (Hence the need to train our minds to think positively – see Chapter 3). Conversely, flow carries us forward through the activity in a timeless kind of bubble where everyday concerns and thoughts are banished. Thankfully, the need to concentrate fully and focus our attention on the activity leaves no room for the banal thoughts that enter our mind while we embark on activities that aren't flow-inducing. Flow excludes all of that irrelevance and enables order to quieten the chaos of our everyday minds. Hence why finding activities which do induce a state of flow and enjoying them regularly is a great way to boost our well-being and enjoy our life more.

As Mihaly Csikszentmihalyi says, "When an activity is thoroughly engrossing, there is not enough attention left over to allow a person to consider either the past or the future, or any other temporarily irrelevant stimuli... leaving aside everything not essential to that game..."

That's why the duration of time tends to be skewed. As the saying goes, 'time flies when you're having fun.'

Grow With The Flow
To Expand Yourself

Pleasure, like happiness, is a fleeting feeling. That's why pleasure alone doesn't enable psychological growth or sustainable well-being, hence why passive activities which generate pleasure aren't always the most enjoyable. In order to grow as people we need to stretch; to challenge and expand ourselves. Fortunately each and every one of us has ample opportunity to do precisely that.

Each time we put our skills to good use, experience 'flow' and achieve a decent result, we boost our own self-confidence and expand ourselves. Furthermore, as outlined in the previous chapter, identifying your strengths and using them as often as possible is well-being booster in itself. But it also enables flow and growth. Each challenge that we face and overcome using our skills makes us feel good and makes us feel capable. That's why investing in goals which put our skills to good use and require focus and concentration, makes for an enjoyable experience. Each time we carry out a task which uses our skills and achieves a goal we are rewarded with a joyful feeling and so we repeat this. In doing so we grow.

As Mihaly Csikszentmihalyi says in his book, "the overwhelming proportion of optimal experiences are reported to occur within sequences of activities that are goal-directed and bounded by rules – activities that require the investment of psychic energy, and that could not be done without the appropriate skills."

And so, by using our skills in activities which provide us with feedback en route to clear goals, we grow with the flow. Conversely, if activities don't have clear goals or feedback, our attention can falter and our quality of experience is diluted.

How to grow with the flow:

- **Participate in activities which provide you with feedback regarding how well you are doing in terms of achieving your goal.** For example, a footballer know that she needs to score a goal and prevent the opposing team from scoring. Each time she kicks the ball, she knows how well she has done and whether she is close to meeting that [quite literal] goal. In other activities, where the goal/feedback is less clear cut (or literal), it's important to know the desired result. For example, if you are creating a collage or painting a mural, you should have a good idea about how you wish it to look when completed. Based on that information, you can know with each positioning of a new image and each fresh brush stroke, whether you are on course or not. In order to optimise the quality of our experiences, we must use our own internal instincts and guidelines to flag up our own good 'moves', and ultimately keep us on track toward our goals.

- **Compete to sharpen your skill, but do so because you enjoy the activity and want to hone and improve your skills rather than to win; you'll enjoy it more.** Competition can be a stimulating challenge and one in which you grow, but not if all that matters is winning.

- **Make sure your component provides a worthy challenge. i.e. ensure that your skills and challenges are matched**. If your skills are mismatched and they are way better than you or your challenge is too difficult; you may perfect your skills during the process (and thus reach your goal) but you'll find that the feedback you get won't be as positive and so the activity will be less enjoyable and more frustrating. Similarly, if you are way better than your opponent, or the challenge is not difficult enough, the activity won't be adequately challenging for you to improve your skills and your enjoyment will also be diluted. Try to get the balance right.

- **Push yourself outside of your comfort zone.** Challenge yourself to do better. Enjoyment is diminished when you repeat an activity at the same level over and over.

- **Enjoy the gratification and self-growth that achieving a goal creates.** Realise that your fresh achievements gained via your new or improved skills have enriched your experience. You are now a better version of yourself; you have grown; you have taken a step forward. When you achieve a goal you are actualising your potential or are one step closer to doing so. Not only that, in practising your skills you are discovering new and better ways or perfecting existing ways of doing things. In doing so, you are growing.

- **Embrace learning.** Optimal experience includes the experience of learning. And through learning we grow. 'nough said.

Choose Absorbing Activities To Boost Enjoyment And Gratification

The activities you choose to fill your wonderful life should be as autotelic as possible. i.e. doing the activity is its own reward, rather than doing it to gain some future reward. Of course, in competitive sports you have goals (to win, to improve, to teach others) but that is not the key reason for doing the activity, you should be doing the activity because you love to do it; because you enjoy it.

This may sound a little contradictory. After all, one of the key pillars of well-being is to have goals and, in order to achieve 'flow', you should have goals and gain feedback in relation to those goals as you undertake an activity. The key definition here is that, while you do need goals and these are important to enable a feeling of accomplishment and achievement (and working towards goals boosts well-being in itself), there is no point in doing an activity purely for that purpose... it must be done for it's own sake too, because you enjoy that activity and get absorbed in it. So, instead of doing something because you feel you have to or just because it will bring you some reward sometime down the line, it's better to do it because you want to and because doing it brings its own reward right now in the very experience of doing it.

> *"When experience is intrinsically rewarding life is justified in the present, instead of being held hostage to a hypothetical future gain."*
> **Mihaly Csikszentmihalyi**

Find Your Sunshine in Life and Work: Do What You Love and Love What You Do

Human beings are happier when it's sunny than when it's rainy (although it does give us a happy feeling when it's chucking it down outside and we're all snuggled and warm inside our homes). However, particularly in the often rain-ridden UK, we need to source our own sunshine by filling our lives with stuff that we love to do, both during our working time and leisure time. Seeing as we only have one life, it's vital that we PRIORITISE OUR PASSION. We must identify what we are passionate about and make time for it so we get to pursue our passion on a regular basis rather than merely fitting it in during the increasingly-sparse spare moments at the end of a weekend. In doing so we can boost our well-being tremendously.

So, about that...

Enjoy Your Work

Unless we have ample funds from wealthy families or lottery wins, the majority of us have to spend a good deal of our lives at work, earning a living.

Work gets a bad press. A lot of this comes down to how you view the very notion of work. The word job signifies duty, obligation and responsibility. Sadly, because it is something we *have* to do, the majority of people see it as a chore; a big time-sapping burden which takes us away from life. If you do something because you have to and not because you want to that is how we see it – as an inconvenience and certainly not as something to be enjoyed. And yet, while we do have to work, many of us, if we really think about it, actually want to work more than we realise. That's why many lottery winners don't actually give up work altogether, because they like it. They don't have to work any more, but they do it because they want to.

Despite this automatically negative space that we slot work into, if we are honest with ourselves, many of us do actually enjoy work, or at least part of it. The variation of what we do is enjoyable. We like being with others and having a laugh/joke/gossip during our working hours; we like working towards goals and completing projects; some of us relish the freedom and flexibility that working from home affords us with, or the time we get to ourselves en route to work (for some people that's the only time they get to themselves). Self-employed people enjoy being their own boss and relish the knowledge that, if something isn't done today, it can be done tomorrow.

Indeed, in his studies on work as flow, Mihaly Csikszentmihalyi discovered that work rather than leisure was in fact the major source of optimal experiences. People reported more flow situations at work than they did in leisure. It seems that this is because work tends to have variety and is made up of various challenges that require concentration and skill to complete. Furthermore, at work we are privy to constant feedback - from ourselves, from our colleagues or competitors and from our managers or our clients. And so it fits that these work-based activities provide 'flow' or optimal experience.

I consider myself to be incredibly blessed. I love what I do. What I do is varied. I split my time between researching, writing, editing, educating (through the content I write), promoting what I've written and learning. I've worked hard to be where I am now – a work from home author and small business founder. I love being self-employed and all that goes with it. I feel empowered and free. I feel I have a purpose and my work life has meaning. I love and get completely immersed in researching and writing and editing and creating. I wake up happy on Monday mornings. Many people don't because they say. 'Hmpf. I have to go to work.' Yes, I have to go to work too. But I'm glad about that. I would do what I do even if I was wealthy enough not to have to earn a living; if my living was already earned I would still write books for fun. (Albeit with many more frequent exotic holidays inbetween).

If you wouldn't do what you do for a living if you didn't have to, you have two choices. You can either:

1. Spend some time figuring out what you'd love to do for a living. Ask yourself this: what would I do if money was no object and if success was guaranteed? List your answers below. Then assess whether that course of action is viable. What steps would you need to take in order to make that happen? Do you have the support needed to make this change? If not how might you get it?

_____

_____

_____

2. Make what you do for a living more enjoyable by making your work activities more engaging. To do this, and especially if your work is not particularly varied, you need to figure out ways that you can maximise concentration on tasks, the opportunity to hone and develop your existing skills, set clear goals and be sure that you have in place methods of getting feedback on how well you are doing. The more challenges you can set within your role and the more skills you utilise, the more enjoyable those tasks will be. You could even figure out ways that you could make certain tasks into a game e.g. getting further, doing more, doing better each time or performing a task within a certain time-scale.

The upside of enjoying work-based activities is that you will be more productive, creative and motivated as a result. That's in contrast to activities that don't require much engagement such as watching TV or socialising with friends.

Indeed, how satisfied you are in your job (or at least how dissatisfied you are not) may surprise you. If you consider what you like about your job (e.g. the people, the tasks themselves, harnessing your skills, the social element, fulfilling a purpose, and so on) and then think about what you don't like about your job (e.g. the pressure/ stress, the conflicts with your boss, the lack of variety or challenge, the lack of recognition or reward), you may be able to make significant changes to make what you like about it outweigh what you dislike. If you are seeking more variety, challenge or recognition or would prefer to have less pressure, talk to someone about it and consider your career options. Then consider how you approach your job and see if you can change the way you think about it, and focus on what you enjoy, create more challenges for yourself within each task you carry out, focus on tasks which fully utilise your core skills and relish the times you are enjoying your work. If you can take the rough with the smooth and focus your attention on the smooth, you'll enjoy your work more.

I am an advocate of self-employdom but you need to have strict guidelines so that you don't overwork/overwhelm your life with work. There are many benefits. You avoid the conflicts with your boss because you don't have one. You are free to spend more time with your family by working around them (I work 9am-3pm and 8-10pm). More and more people are taking this option, but it doesn't come without its immense stresses, strains and pressures. Being self-employed is NOT the easy option as you leave the safety net of a regular pay-packet for the big unknown. You don't get paid if you are sick or go on holiday. The buck stops with you and you can experience cabin fever. I believe the benefits far outweigh the obstacles though. Otherwise I wouldn't have been self-employed for the past 14 years.

Considering the status quo assumption that work is a negative experience, why do studies show that the majority of flow/optimum experiences happen at work rather than when we are chilling out at home? Unstructured leisure time can be enjoyable but studies have shown that it is less enjoyable than we think. We end up tired and filled with apathy. Not motivated to do much. We passively watch sportsmen and women play in stadiums rather than play ourselves.

We listen to music instead of making music. We admire other people's art hung on walls instead of creating our own art. I guess if we get too passive, relaxation becomes lethargy which makes our downtime rather dull.

Those who devote at least some of their leisure time to active activities such as playing sport, making music or building stuff end up enjoying their lives more.

"The future will belong not only to the educated man,
but to the man who is educated to use his leisure wisely,"
C.K. Brightbil

Enjoy Your Life:
Bring Your Own Sunshine

Enjoying life more isn't merely about improving the quality of experiences, it's about relishing each and every experience that we have. It's about SAVOURING those experiences. Whether that's eating an ice cream, breathing in that first aroma of coffee in the morning, catching your child chuckling to herself, feeling the warm sun on your skin, taking a morning walk or being in the company of a good friend. It's important to savour small experiences as well as big ones; absorb every drop of beauty, pleasure and positive emotion. The next Chapter on Mindfulness will help you to savour each and every moment, and any activity where you reminisce on positive past events will help you to savour life more too. The key is to do something, anything, that brings you a burst of positive emotion, even if it only lasts for a few moments. The more moments you can savour, the more that positive feeling will spiral through and impact your life.

Your aim here is to do more of what you love, less of what you don't (or make it more enjoyable) and change anything left that you don't enjoy, where possible.

The point is to get out there and do something. When I was a child I used to watch a programme called *Why Don't You*. It had a catchy theme tune, "Why Don't You, stop watching TV, get out of your bed and go and do something less boring instead." We watch too much TV, play too many computer games and spend not enough time going out there into the world and experiencing stuff for REAL. The virtual always-on world has replaced the outdoors and the imaginative. Stretch yourself, take part, get your hands dirty. Just join in. How? You could go to evening classes, join a club or group or association, volunteer, mentor – try new things and do more of the things you know you love to do; the activities that uplift you. Just get out there and get active.

Over the following pages you'll get the opportunity to list everything that uplifts you. This might include a phone call with a certain person, a certain piece of music, eating ice cream, an activity such as dancing, laughing with your children, walking the dog in the field near your house, ice skating... whatever you love to do. Ready?...

"People who have fun are 20 times as likely to feel happy,"
Gretchen Rubin

- **Play more. Source more fun.** Grab a pen and write three lists (See below). First is your **FUN LIST:** source and brainstorm feel good fun activities that you enjoy which will provide you with the utmost satisfaction. Fun-loving participants of FUN are happier and more energised, obviously. Additionally though, after participating in some proper fun, you'll feel more able to crack on with your to-do list. Fun is thus productive.

  So, what do you love to do? Get scribbling and write non-stop for a good 10 minutes if you can. What topics and activities interest you and get you excited which you could talk endlessly about/do for hours? What are your favourite smells/sounds/sights? How might you experience more of those through fun activities?

- **Now jot down a list of engaging activities that you find gratifying yet challenging**. This is your **ENGAGING/ CHALLENGING LIST.** These activities should require skills and concentration. They could be micro activities which fill gaps in the day or activities which take a bit more planning or longer periods of participation. You may find that some activities belong on both your FUN list and your ENGAGING and CHALLENGING list. Get scribbling. Write down every thing you love to do as you ponder those questions over the coming week. Put a star next to the ones that you love to do the most. Which of these make you feel really good and satisfy or energise you the most? You'll be scheduling them into your FLOURISH PLANNER later on.

- **Now write your BACK THEN LIST including 10 activities you loved doing when you were 10 or 11 years old.** Tap into the enthusiasm that you had when you were a child. This is likely not to be too dissimilar, but there may be some activities (like rolling down grassy hills or jumping through sprinklers with friends or similar) that you don't tend to spend time doing now.

MY FUN LIST	MY ENGAGING/CHALLENGING LIST	BACK THEN
e.g.		
Dancing	Writing	Reading
Socialising	Reading	Drawing
Fishing	Meditating	Playing Netball
Camping	List-making/planning	Climbing Trees
Eating Out	Playing Netball	Building Dens
		Performing

MY FUN LIST	MY ENGAGING/CHALLENGING LIST	BACK THEN

- Jot down what the other people in your family love to do.

  What does your other half LOVE to do?

  _____

  _____

  _____

  _____

  What do your children LOVE to do?

  _____

  _____

  _____

  _____

- **Keep a photographic journal of enjoyable experiences and stuff that makes you smile.** This encourages you to notice what activities, places, people, experiences, products bring you joy. Whether it's a piece of art, a view you see on your way to work, a smiling face of a loved-one, or a frothy coffee made with your new cappuccino maker, record whatever brings out the smile in you and you'll seek out more of the same so that you can really savour each moment, savour life more by doing more of what makes you smile. (A visually account of stuff that makes you feel good is also useful to leaf through when you need a boost).

- **Open a 'fun' account or money-box.** Not a savings account per se, but an account (or money-box) in which you deposit between 1-10% of your monthly income to spend on YOU, to spend on having FUN, to spend on fun activities that you and your family enjoy, whether that's fishing, cycling, ice-skating, netball... be it having a massage and facial, eating out with friends, buying books or magazines to read. You may already do this, but making a point of putting aside money specifically for free time activities will make you focus more on what you do and how you do it.

- **Watch less TV.** The average Westerner spends between three to five hours plonked on their sofas watching television every single day. Make, bake, build, create, learn, read... just do anything other than watching TV or playing computer games.

- **Explore your local attractions.** Get out there. Make time for mini-adventures.

- **Step boldly outside of your comfort zone.** Stimulate your life by being brave. Give yourself a nudge towards the unfamiliar. Challenge yourself to do something you wouldn't ordinarily do, something that stretches your own boundaries and limitations. This does three things – it invigorates and stimulates you, gives you the means to live in the moment/appreciate the now and it kicks complacency into touch. In life, as soon as you rest on your laurels something often happens to smash that safe zone apart. Far better to do it on your terms using your own courage. So go out there and splash cold water in the face of your life. It'll invigorate you, fill you with confidence and give you a wonderful sense of empowerment and achievement. And don't think 'I can't do that.' You'll create a self-fulfilling prophecy of being unable to do stuff. Try it. You can. Learning sparks interest and excitement and boosts positive emotion too. Meeting new people, visiting new places, playing new games, trying new activities, all of these predispose you to feeling happier than those who merely stick to what they know and never stray from their routine.

- **Know that failure is fun.** Mistakes are vital lessons. The only real failure is failing to learn from mistakes and repeating them down the line. Learning lessons the hard way is proven to be a better way of learning. Because those lessons stick.

- **Create engines of happiness for yourself,** i.e. activities which stretch you at first but then constantly stimulate you each time you add a log to the fire by doing them again.

- **Join a club.** Partake in group activity. Studies reveal that well-being can be boosted significantly when you participate in activities with others who share that common interest. Tell people about your club or flourishing activities at: www.Facebook.com/groups/theflourishers

We spend, as adults, a third of our waking life alone, all by ourselves. The author of *Flow* seems to think that being alone is, in most cases, depressing and lonely and rubbish. I disagree. I love my own company. Maybe this is due to my being an only child? Maybe it's because I've chosen to work from home on my own for so long (14 years) and relish every moment. I love a full and bustling household with friends and family but also cherish when it's just me because I am free from distraction and interruption, free to be with my own thoughts.

What activities do you like to do on your own and which do you prefer to do with others? Have you ever tried going to the cinema or doing an activity that you'd normally do with other people by yourself? Perhaps you should give it a whirl. You might enjoy it?

Flourish Toolkit:
Pick 'n Mix (100 Well-being
Boosting Activities Checklist)

Sometimes, as adults, we choose activities as a means to kill some time, rather than to fill some time. This is the result of boredom. The best activities to fill your free time are those which involve and improve skills and therefore result in self-development. Truly engaging activities will require an element of concentration, goal-setting and feedback so that you can completely immerse yourself in the activity too. However, sometimes, we need a break, we need to partake in non-engaging activities which still make us feel good, such as luxuriating in a hot bubble bath while singing at the top of our voices, or eating at a restaurant with friends and family. If you can aim to get a good mix of both kinds of feel-good activities, i.e. active engaging ones which involve an element of mastery and passive relaxing ones which don't, you will be filling your free time in a very positive way and, as a result, you will feel refreshed and motivated, and flourish.

Some simple activities, such as walking for instance, can be particularly engaging if you do more than simply walk out of the door with no real aim. For instance, if you select goals involving destination, route, places to stop at, topics and new ideas to talk about and explore en route, you can optimise the experience of walking and turn it into a 'flow' activity.

Living an activity-based family life with optimal experience at its centre has long-lasting positive effects on children too. If a child sees that dad tends to spend most of his free time in front of the TV or playing computer games/texting and passively vegetating in his armchair, they'll regard grown-ups as boring and will look primarily to their peers to spend time having fun with. Conversely, if you build fun activities into your free time, and enjoy tinkering in the garage, cooking, gardening, playing sports, mum and dad will be viewed as worth spending time with.

Furthermore, being an engagingly active family makes it clear to children what is expected from them in terms of the level of family interaction and provides a sub-conscious feeling of security. This is because, in demonstrably living a life in which enjoyment of the present is focused on, pressures about the future aren't the main preoccupations (and, certainly at teenager level, the pressure about doing well enough to get into uni or to get a good job don't need to be focused on any more than they already are within normal society). Teaching our kids to enjoy the moment and optimise experience evidently has a very positive effect.

Once a week or month plan to have a family adventure, whether that's visiting an aquarium or going on a long bike ride and having a pub lunch or hiring horses to ride on horseback, go sailing, visit a farm or transform your allotment. This could be the first or last Saturday in every month, for example.

Here's a checklist of 100 well-being boosting activities to choose from and schedule into your planner. They can be done alone or with others. Whichever activities you pick and mix, enjoy each moment of each experience and you'll be living a flourishing life.

*Note: refer back to your own fun-list on page 125. Add to this pick 'n mix checklist any activities from your personal fun list which are not included.

Flourish Pick 'n Mix:
100 Well-being Boosting Activities

1. Go to the circus or learn to juggle.
2. Fly a kite.
3. Bake a cake.
4. Read a book that makes you smile (to yourself or to your child). You could try some children's literature. *Add your preferred reading material to the Mood-Boosting Flourishers Reading List on page 86.
5. Read a magazine.
6. Start or join a book club.
7. Visit the park. Swing high.
8. Draw or paint a picture or mural. Get the whole family involved.
9. Create something new from recycled objects.
10. Write a story. Rather than merely transmit and pass on information, create it instead.
11. Write a letter, poem, diary, song or blog. Just get scribbling.
12. Build a den.
13. Build an intricate rock garden.
14. Start a community garden.
15. Climb a tree.
16. Plant a tree or a mini orchard.
17. Get an allotment or plant an edible fruit and vegetable garden.
18. Visit somewhere you've never been before. Look at free family magazines you get in the library and circle potential adventures and activities.
19. Make/record some music.
20. Play an instrument.
21. Listen to music. Don't just hear the music, really listen to it. Dim the lights, remove distractions and pay attention to each note. Then you'll truly experience the tune. *Add your favourite mood-boosting tunes to the Flourishers Playlist on page 134.
22. Find a mountain and go climb it.
23. Dance and/or sing.
24. Put on a show (puppet show, song and dance performance).
25. Go sailing.
26. Go fishing.
27. Go camping.
28. Go for a long walk (with pub lunch at the end?)
29. Bounce on a trampoline.
30. Play chess.
31. Have a picnic or tea party.
32. Meditate.
33. Practice yoga or pilates. Try Yoga-Nidra for something new (yoga/painting).
34. Make a smoothie or home-made lemonade.
35. Play a board game.
36. Knit, weave or sew .
37. Debate on a range of topics.
38. Solve a mental puzzle, such as a crossword.
39. Make up your own crosswords.
40. Interpret musical notation.
41. Create a vision board or gratitude board.
42. Create a mosaic snapshot of your family by selecting photos through the ages.
43. Make a scrapbook.
44. Make your own birthday cards.
45. Write a family chronicle by looking into your family history and examining your family tree.
46. Visit a farm and pay attention.
47. Notice nature. Take macro photos. Breathe in the fresh air.
48. Make a CD of photos for your friends.
49. Consider ways to be your own boss.
50. Ride on horseback.
51. Visit an aquarium.
52. Visit the zoo. Just enjoying the sen-

sory delight of seeing a giraffe tend to its young is engaging in itself.

53. Visit the races (horse/motocross/car...)
54. Go on a long bike ride with a pub lunch as your reward.
55. Go swimming.
56. Fix a broken engine or item.
57. Doodle or paint a picture.
58. Find a grassy hill and roll down it.
59. Cook a meal.
60. Build your own garden swing.
61. Go foraging in the countryside for wild food
62. Go foraging at the local dump for someone else's rubbish you can transform into your own treasure.
63. Go on a treasure hunt.
64. Play football, netball, basketball...
65. Have a massage/facial
66. Go to a restaurant but optimise the experience by paying attention to every mouthful and really tasting each flavour rather than barely noticing what you're putting in your mouth. Talk about taste sensations. Relish the experience of eating.
67. Learn something new. Do something you have never done before.
68. Go ice skating or roller blading
69. Go abseiling.
70. Volunteer or mentor/coach someone.
71. Do a sponsored activity to fund-raise or arrange a fund-raising event.
72. Do a random act of kindness. Have a kindness competition with other family members.
73. Make a list of the activities you would do if you only had one week to live. Then do them.
74. Go on a photography expedition.
75. Visit a photography exhibition.
76. Have a family hula-hooping competition.
77. Re-arrange the furniture, play with and transform your surroundings in some fashion.
78. Weed the garden and visit the garden centre to get some new plants.
79. Go orienteering.
80. Sprout your own alfalfa seeds.
81. Go rambling.
82. Go bowling.
83. Join a choir.
84. Do some dance-fitness – Bodyjam, Zumba, ShBam or try Burlesque via www.vieolette.co.uk
85. Go canoeing.
86. Have a bush craft adventure in your local woods.
87. Do some skipping or hula-hopping.
88. Go trekking with Llamas.
89. Use your skills to solve a problem.
90. Fire-walk.
91. Print your own t-shirts or customise your clothes.
92. Have a Lego building challenge.
93. Paint each others' faces. See how creative you can be. Score each others out of 10.
94. Go to the library and immerse yourself in books (peace and quiet).
95. Have a luxurious soak in the bath or tuneful invigorating shower.
96. Make and edit a home movie from one of your family adventures (or a whole bunch of them, then have a screening, complete with popcorn). Reminiscing on positive memories is great for our well-being.
97. Record your parents earliest recollections and share them with your children.
98. Have an egg carriage race amongst your family with prizes for x, y and z.
99. Visit a pottery and make something.
100. Book and prepare for an adventure of a lifetime. See www.momentumadventure.com

Or... Do something spontaneous :-)

Of course there is something to be said for spontaneity. All this scheduling of activities is proven to be incredibly beneficial (enabling you to squeeze more of what you love doing into your life and consequently enjoying life more)... yet it is still nice to wake up on a weekend with NO PLANS WHATSOEVER and just go with the flow – do whatever you feel like doing at that moment, to be spontaneous in your experiences.

Mood Boosting Flourishers Reading List

Immersing yourself in a good book is a great mood-boosting activity in itself. You might think reading is more passive than active but it is actually one of the most engaging activities which enables relaxation, escapism and flow. Reading is also a great de-stressing activity as Mindlab International Research revealed recently that reading reduced stress by 67%. While you might think the only skill reading requires is to be able to read, it also requires concentration. What is particularly interesting is that reading is also therapeutic – if you choose the right book. Indeed, doctors have recently drawn up a list of 27 'mood-boosting' books which promote well-being to help lift people out of depression, soothe anxiety and reduce stress. The list has been distributed by GPs as part of a 'Books on Prescription' scheme, supported by the Department for Health.

Mood Boosting Flourishers Reading List

1. *The Beach Café* by Lucy Diamond
2. *Being Human* by Neil Astley
3. *The Big Over Easy* by Jasper Fforde
4. *Big Stone Gap* by Adriana Trigiani
5. *Cider with Rosie* by Laurie Lee
6. *Couch Fiction* by Philippa Perry
7. *Haroun and the Sea of Stories* by Salman Rushdie
8. *Hector and the Search for Happiness* by Francois Lelord
9. *Life According to Lubka* by Laurie Graham
10. *Life with the Lid Off* by Nicola Hodgkinson
11. *A Little History of the World* by E. H. Gombrich
12. *Major Pettigrew's Last Stand* by Helen Simonson
13. *Men at Work* by Mike Gayle
14. *Notes from a Small Island* by Bill Bryson
15. *Prodigal Summer* by Barbara Kingsolver
16. *The Pursuit of Love* by Nancy Mitford
17. *Smoke and Mirrors* by Neil Gaiman
18. *A Spot of Bother* by Mark Haddon
19. *Tackling Life* by Charlie Oatway
20. *That Awkward Age* by Roger McGough
21. *To the Moon and Back* by Jill Mansell
22. *Trouble on the Heath* by Terry Jones
23. *A Winter Book* by Tove Jansson
24. *Stop What You're Doing and Read This*
    - Various contributors
25. *Tales of the City* by Armistead Maupin
26. *Waterlog* by Roger Deakin
27. *The Secret Garden* by Frances Hodgson Burnett

Mood Boosting Music Playlist

Music is emotive. It takes us back to happy (or sad) places. It is incredibly powerful in that sense to evoke emotion and trigger feelings. There are some songs that are inherently happy.

The Flourish Handbook has worked with musicologists to create a 12-track playlist of mood-boosting music. Stick this on and it WILL make you feel happier.
http://www.youtube.com/playlist?list=PLLa4kbM0s54NnG2otwn_lxHqVURZP7gp1

So what are the criteria for a feel good song? Well, according to research by RaRa.com, the melody should be played in a major rather than a minor key predictable with a punchy beat and fast pace and the voice should be high-pitched. Harmonies and acapella also work well. So says Dr Lewis who looked for music that stimulates the limbic and reward systems - areas of the brain responsible for generating emotions and sensations of pleasure.

Of course feel-good music really is subjective and depends on the individual and the memory or feeling they associate with a particular song. I like artists that you don't like and vice versa. However, any song that 'reminds you of a time when you were blissfully happy' has the power to put you back in that mood.

The Flourisher Playlist

http://www.youtube.com/playlist?list=PLLa4kbM0s54NnG2otwn_lxHqVURZP7gp1
1. Dion and the Belmonts – Runaround Sue
2. Martha & The Muffins - Echo Beach
3. Gorillaz - Feel Good Inc
4. Daft Punk - Get Lucky
5. The Levellers – What a Beautiful Day
6. Outkast - Hey Ya
7. Corinne Bailey Rae – Go Put Your Records On

8. The Mamas & The Papas - California Dreamin
9. Stevie Wonder – Part-Time Lover
10. Bob Marley – Three Little Birds
11. Beyonce – Love On Top
12. Belinda Carlisle - Heaven Is A Place On Earth
13. FPI Project – Everybody (All Over The World)

Join The Flourishers group on Facebook https://www.facebook.com/groups/theflourishers/ to add your own suggestions of tunes and books to boost positive emotion and share the activities that you do to boost your well-being.

To Do List and Planner

Enter a contest where I can use my skills

Make my own FEEL GOOD reading list

Make my own FEEL GOOD ♫♪ music playlist ☺

Plan a career change / ways to make my job more engaging

Open a "FUN" account or money box £

FLOURISH PLANNER (ongoing)

Schedule in:
- Some FUN activities, some ENGAGING activities that harness your skills/strengths and some RELAXING activities including those which each family member LOVES to do.
- Some activities that you used to love when you were 10 or 11 years old.
- An activity that you've never done before that requires learning.

Chapter 6

MONTH SIX:
Be Mindful and Practice Mindfulness

Find Your Inner Peace and Equip Yourself to Gain More Control Over Your Life

"Mindfulness is about waking up to your life"

In order to flourish in this – our one and only life – we must cherish every moment that we possibly can, we must revel in this time in our life, pay attention to what is happening around us, appreciate the seasons, the time of day, what we can hear, see, feel, touch and taste... Of course, this is much easier said than done. With most of us living at 100mph, often on autopilot and, therefore, not actively engaged or even in control of what we're doing, relishing each moment of our lives is not an easy process at all. As we hurry frantically from one thing to the next, scuttling stressed and exhausted through life as rat race participants or busy parents, our time-starved energy-deprived selves can find it difficult to stop the hamster wheel. But stop we must. And this is where the practice of mindfulness comes in to play. Mindfulness is a major enabler. It's a tool to help us manage and cope better with life.

Scientific studies have revealed that mindfulness helps reduce stress, anxiety and depression; boost the immune system, improve pain-management, sleep and concentration; increase positive emotions, lift mood, reduce rumination and improve quality of life. The benefits are evident. Mindfulness is indeed a mood-lifting, stress-busting, mind-calming, concentration-elevating, habit-breaking, pain-reducing, wellbeing-boosting memory-enhancing practice of wonderfulness.

Yet, with our uber-packed lifestyles, how can we stop to smell the roses? Well lovely reader-of-this -book, I shall show you exactly how. Apart from devoting time this month to practicing mindfulness, your aim is to build this practice into your daily life going forwards. Remember, we are working our way towards a wondrous part of your Flourish Toolkit – the Ultimate Flourish Planner, and that will include dedicated time to practice mindfulness in short 5-15 minute bursts a few times per week. In doing so you can gradually build mindfulness into your mindset – it will become second nature – and your new mindful self will subsequently enjoy life more, deal with stress better and flourish. Yippeee!

So what precisely is mindfulness? Is it about relaxing and chilling out? Nope. 'Fraid not. It can make you feel relaxed, but that is not at its centre. Relaxation is about switching off whereas mindfulness is about "switching on to you."It's about slowing down and paying attention so that you can notice, observe and feel more of what is going on in this very moment here... and this one... each moment noticed, appreciated, and absorbed. It's about cultivating AWARENESS about what is happening around you and within you at any given moment, so that you can regain control over your fast-paced life and the choices you make.

As Cheryl A Rezek explains in her book, *Mindfulness: How the mindful approach can help you towards a better life*: "Mindfulness cultivates calm, confidence and control and helps you to feel more stable and resilient. Mindful people feel ready to take on whatever life throws at them."

Yep, mindfulness is indeed a very nifty life-management tool. It simply equips you with a method of dealing better with whatever life flings your way. When your mind is still, it is easier to see what is good and present. When your mind is anxious, it is easier to see what is negative and missing.

Different people deal with stress and situations in different ways. However, for the most part, our bodies react in a specific way by going into survival sympathetic mode. When stressed out, our bodies/brains do not realise that a situation is not of real danger to us, but react in a way that can cause more harm than good by redirecting energy from vital areas (such as our immune system, digestive system, decision-making part of our brain). It releases stress hormones, cortisol and adrenaline which is much like sitting in a car, revving the engine then slamming on the brakes over and over – utterly pointless. This reaction to a stressful situation achieves nothing – you get nowhere, you merely exhaust the vehicle, waste fuel and wear out the brakes. Evidently – stress sucks! However, there are exercises we can do to prevent this natural reaction to stress, regain control, calm down and equip ourselves better to deal with any eventuality, no matter how harsh.

Be Present in the Present

1. **Regain control**. When others are preoccupied – nodding yet not really listening or paying attention to what you're saying, that's annoying right? But we do that to ourselves all the time. Thinking 'ooh, I really ought to exercise more, go to bed earlier, drink more water and nodding, but then being preoccupied and dismissing the good intention as quickly as it popped into our minds. We also dismiss most moments in time as we are pre-occupied and distracted, thinking about other stuff. We wolf down our food without savouring each mouthful. We end up re-reading a page of our book because we were thinking about stuff we need to do; we don't pay full attention to someone who is telling us something because our mind is elsewhere, focused instead on what we need to do or where we need to be. We are, as such, out of control, constantly pre-occupied, distracted, unaware as life flies by. Where did the time go? We wonder. It was right there, under our noses. If only we'd taken the time to notice it.

   • **Stop being pre-occupied for at least 15 minutes each day during this month**. Sit silently and quietly so that you can regain control, become aware of what is happening internally and externally in any given moment and communicate with the universe. When people say - "empty your mind," "clear your mind," that's tough. Trying to resist thinking doesn't tend to work. The way to still your mind is to notice your thoughts and let them in and then … just watch them go. So try this: Close your eyes and watch your thoughts appear. As you notice them they will most probably dissipate. By paying attention to your thoughts and letting them in rather than trying not to think at all you will gradually be able to have a clear mind for 20 seconds or so at a time. The feeling of being in full control of your mind and being able to command it to be still is empowering. This empowerment makes you realise that you can switch your thoughts from negative to positive, just as you can still your mind at any given moment. It takes practice but it's worth it.

- **Pick one of the mindfulness pick n mix activities** from the list on pages 144-146 to practice during or after this 15 minutes of quiet still time.

2. **Embrace life warts-and-all**. Savour the good moments and the bad moments and you'll feel better equipped to deal with all that life entails. The fact is, life is often difficult. It just is. There will be tough times. FACT. So how are you going to deal with them? When something wonderful or terrible happens:

- **Stay with that moment.** Ponder how you will deal with it. Don't dilute the moment by hiding it away, putting on a brave face, ignoring it and consequently diluting it. Instead focus on this moment, be it tough and awkward or pleasant and uplifting. If the moment causes pain or sadness, embrace it. Those feelings are part of you, part of being a human-being. If you opt instead to deny that pain and ignore or sweep over that suffering you are denying who you are. Focus on it, accept it, consider what it has taught you about life, about yourself and about how you can cope. Cry, laugh, write down or record your thoughts, but never ignore it. Stay with the moment and then let it pass, equipped with the knowledge that you can deal with it.

"Life is not happy or sad, good or bad, easy or hard, it is all of these things in different measures at different times, but always together,"
Cheryl A Rezek

3. **Make better choices and respond better.** Choose how to respond and deal with stuff instead of reacting in a way that doesn't serve you well. Life is unpredictable. In the next few minutes, hours, weeks, years something unexpected is likely to happen. Who knows what tomorrow brings. But we can make the most of our lives by living in this very moment – noticing this moment now, before it's gone, and determining how we shall be within it by making better choices. Ask yourself how you react when something annoys you? When someone cuts you up, parks in 'your' parking space, drives too fast (or slow), criticises you, lights a fire in the summer when you have all the windows open or washing out (grrr... pet hate). Do you slam those windows shut, cursing and muttering, stomp downstairs, post a rant on FB and simmer in a grump for a while? (I have been guilty of this myself in my pre-mindful days). Do you feel cross, frowny and subsequently get a headache? Do you flare up in a defensive rage when criticised? I know I have done. And does this reaction make what has happened any less annoying? Does it dilute the problem or magnify it? Far better to choose to deal with each moment in a positive way. For example, by thinking that driver who drove or parked inappropriately has probably just been laughed at or criticised or told to hurry up or in a grump, the fire will pass. Make the most of a bad situation and go for a walk or do something you wouldn't have had the opportunity to do if this hadn't have happened. Take criticism on board. It may not be a criticism. It may be a truth. And seeing a truth

(even if it's not one you wish to hear) can be very positive as it can act as a motivator and catalyst for change. For example, I've always been quite untidy but having been criticised for this I now try harder to keep things tidy, a positive step which has given me so much more mind space.

It's empowering when you choose not to react negatively to petty annoyances. Instead of being default 'rant', try being what I call default 'sing'. So you change your default reaction to 'lalalaaa, not going to react to this' and you choose to think about something else, breath deeply and go on your merry way instead of reacting negatively. Choosing to react in a default 'sing' way is empowering because it helps you enjoy your life more. If you rant constantly you affect yourself and those you've ranted to and it doesn't change anything. It doesn't make whatever you're ranting about go away or be any less annoying, because what's done is done. In fact, reacting negatively actually magnifies it and makes it more annoying, and can even attract more annoyances towards you.

The past cannot be changed. The future cannot be predicted. The present though – aha – we can have an element of control over that – so by choosing how to deal with each moment – by choosing to take a deep breath, consider something happier and move on instead of choosing to get grumpy or cross when something petty (in the grand scheme of things) happens you can **make each moment better.** How wonderful is that? Conversely, if a moment of pain or loss happens that is not petty (you feel sad about the loss of someone close to you) embrace it and work with it; have a good cry, go for a walk, phone a friend, listen to music, think about how you are a better person for having known him/her. Don't ignore pain, embrace it. But do ignore petty annoyances. By being mindful you'll recognise the difference. (Notably listening to music, breathing in and out mindfully, phoning a friend and choosing to take a walk or a shower... each of these choices work well as a reaction/response choice whether you are dealing with a petty annoyance or a deeply-felt sadness. Better these choices than ranting, shouting, smoking or drinking, for instance).

4. **De-stress yourself and remove anxiety.** As mentioned above, it's important to feel aware of the moment and decide how you'd like to respond. For example, if you are feeling worried or stressed out, rather than getting annoyed or cross with yourself or someone else, acknowledge that moment and focus on your breathing, dissipate the feeling of worry or stress by choosing to be mindful and take appropriate action. You might try the following:

   • **Feel grounded and secure.** Remove your shoes and socks and place your feet firmly on the ground. Notice how the skin of your feet feels against the floor or carpet. Notice how strong and sturdy the floor is. Be aware of the touch point where your foot contacts the floor and feel how stable this makes you feel. See this as a point of stability. Notice that feeling of being grounded, being safe, and feeling calm. Allow that grounded stable feeling to slowly move up your body.

   • **Focus on the rhythm of your breathing**. Breath naturally. Breath in for the count of five and out for the count of five. Place your hand on your abdomen and notice your hand moving upwards and downwards as you breathe inwards and outwards. Focus your mind on that rhythmic movement until you feel calm and in control.

5. **Notice more and enjoy life more.** Rather than watch your child run about on the football pitch in between chatting to other mums and texting, notice the excitement in her eyes when she manages that tough tackle. Experience the glee in his face when you watch him chasing his friends. Breath that moment in, take a snapshot of it in your mind, bottle it and cherish it. (You can even replay that moment as a "reason to be grateful" in the future whenever you might be having a glum moment).

6. **Give yourself a break.** Stop beating yourself up when you make mistakes. Human beings make mistakes. It's what we do.

Mistakes are such important learning tools. Become friends with yourself and be glad to know you and be you. There may be things you've done which you aren't proud of but, as long as you know what those are and know you will behave differently next time, you've learned from that mistake. It was worthwhile. So forgive yourself. You're all right you are.

- Write down the following, it'll take a few seconds to do so but the benefits of doing so will last a whole lot longer:

I am healthy, happy and accept me for all that I am ♡

❤

_____

_____

_____

❤ Flourish Toolkit ❤

PICK N MIX MINDFULNESS TECHNIQUES TO PRACTICE

- **Listen to music**. Focus all of your attention on every bar: listen intently to the melody, now focus on the instruments, become aware of every single note.
- **Make your lunch in a thoroughly attentive way**. Notice each item you use, slow the process down. Be aware of what you can see, touch, the textures of the food you are using, how it feels when you slice a knife through the soft bread, what it smells like, what you can hear whilst you prepare your food. Notice if your mind wanders and where it wanders to. Notice your breathing.

- **Savour taste**. Eat some chocolate (Yay!) First just take a bite as you would normally and carry on doing what you'd normally do, thinking about something else or doing something else as you chew – hardly noticing it, just the occasional bit of yummyness. Now repeat but this time don't chew for a moment and notice the flavour as you slowly start chewing. Pay attention to the taste and keep your chewing action really slow. Savour every moment of that mouthful. Notice the difference in taste? Experience? Sensation?

- **Water your garden but notice every single thing you look at slowly in intense detail.** See your garden in all its technicolour glory, the bark of the tree, the petals, the pollen. Watch ever drop of water soak into the soil and the droplets stick to the leaves. Watch the movement of the plants. Notice everything. Be aware of each plant and how it stands next to another plant. Now close your eyes and listen to each and every sound you can hear, focus on the sounds nearby and the sounds far away. Close your eyes, listen. Open your eyes, look.

- **Have a shower.** Notice the droplets of water as they land on your skin, taste the water, feel the sensation of the water on your skin, not just the temperature of it, but how it feels.

- **Pay attention to what you can hear.** Focus on listening. What sounds are you noticing as you sit or stand quietly still? First listen closely to sounds nearby. Tweeting birds, cars driving past in the distance, trees swaying in the wind, laughter? Did you notice those sounds a moment ago? Consider whether they are loud or soft, gentle, distracting, familiar or soothing, from nature or man? Next focus on sounds that you can hear from far away. Focus your attention back on the close sounds nearby, then the sound of you breathing, of your stomach rumbling, your internal sounds.

- **Experience walking, not just plodding along but really walking.** Notice how the ground feels underneath your feet, how hard it feels (or soft and spongy if walking on grass). Next focus on the movement of your foot and your ankle as it lifts off the ground and then steps down in rhythm. Focus on that rhythm and how your body feels. Focus all of your attention on the parts of your body as you walk and the rhythm of your movement. Next focus on your surroundings and look in detail at one object and another. Look at how each object is positioned and how its colours and textures contrast with other objects within the environment. Next focus on you and how you fit within this environment and how you impact it. Focus on your breathing and its rhythm and feel how you flow through this world, from one place to another so freely.

- **Breath mindfully.** Focus on your breathing. Don't breathe forcefully, just breathe naturally as you always would. Try abdominal rather than shallow breaths using bottom not top of lungs. Use a script for mindful breathing meditation, such as the one that can be found here: http://www.easy-meditation-for-beginners.com/meditation-script.html. Try this body focus meditation to release tension: http://www.youtube.com/watch?v=dbLzoOIuhhs. Alternatively, spend a few minutes merely counting and noticing the rhythm of your breathing and the movement of your hand as you place it on your abdomen. Count 'in, 2, 3, 4' on the inbreath, then count 'out, 2, 3, 4' on the outbreath. Try to practice one of these mindful breathing exercises for five minutes on a daily basis and you will reduce any tension in your mind and body. You'll find yourself better able to respond positively to what life throws your way, boost your concentration and resilience.

- **Release tension by tightening and relaxing the key muscle groups in your body.** Try this 10 minute meditation: http://www.youtube.com/watch?v=SGR-hB0Twro and, in doing so you'll be refuelling your depleted emotional energy reserves and releasing stress simultaneously.

Mindfulness enables us to savour and better enjoy moments, good food, good times, sounds, sights and feelings. It acts as an emotional energy pit stop.

Mindfulness builds patience and tolerance. It enables us to see light in darkness, positive in negative. It brings balance, acceptance of pain and a greater resilience to deal with it. Mindfulness enables us to value each and every moment and experience, whether pleasant or painful.

FLOURISH PLANNER (ongoing)

Schedule in:
- Daily 5 minute mindful breathing exercise
- Daily 5-10 minutes sitting quietly to regain control and become aware.
- Daily or weekly 15 minute mindful exercise from the Pick N Mix of Mindfulness list (stopping preoccupation and distractions on focusing on being in the moment).

Printable Quotes... to cut out n stick up

"A wise old owl sat on an oak;

the more he saw the less he spoke;

the less he spoke the more he heard;

why aren't we like that wise old bird?"

"Courage is what it takes to

stand up and speak;

courage is also what it takes to

sit down and listen."

Winston Churchill

Part 3

Positive Relationships

Chapter 7

MONTH SEVEN:
Make Family Relationships and Friendships Flourish

Cherish and Relish Family and Friendships

*"Connections are like trampolines. The tighter
they are, the higher you'll bounce,"*
Jane Wurwand

Positive relationships with other people contributes massively to our level of well-being and mitigates stress. If you have at least one close long-term friendship plus a relationship network of five or more key 'confidantes' you are, according to studies, more likely to describe yourself as "very happy". Having someone (or something) who is always pleased to see you and who you are always pleased to see is a vital contributor to happiness, as is having people to rely on for emotional support.

One of the founders of positive psychology, Christopher Peterson, once defined what positive psychology is about as "other people." Certainly, strong social bonds and connections with other people serve us on a variety of levels. They essentially provide us with a sense of belonging, self-esteem and identity. They also offer us a level of support with is comforting, a network in which to confide, give and receive empathy. Interaction and communication with other people is a mood-lifting activity which has the power to boost positive emotions. Other people, and our communication with them, evidently, plays a critical role in making us feel happy or unhappy. People contribute to our best and worst times, our happiest and most painful moments. Other people are therefore the prime source of both our positive and negative feelings. Our relationships with others and who we choose to befriend are therefore paramount to our level of well-being.

You see, while having close friendships and a strong social network in itself helps us to flourish, *who* we choose to connect with is also crucial. According to James H Fowler and Nicholas A Christakis, authors of *Connected,* each happy friend increases your probability of being happy by 9%. So who's on your team?

1. **Hang out and spend time with happy positive people.** Moods are contagious, officially so. The scientific name given to the notion of someone lifting us up or bringing us down and thus dictating our mood through their own, is "emotional contagion". Avoid being infected by negativity by spending time with positive people.

   - **Declutter your social relationships.** Spend time with people you are enthusiastic about seeing who are enthusiastic about seeing you, those who lift you up and make you feel good. People who believe in you, encourage and support you and make you smile/ laugh/happy. Create, build and maintain a network of these kinds of people and do all you can to help them. Conversely, avoid spending time with those who bring you down, toxic people who pollute you with their negativity. Avoid people, activities and thoughts which drag you down.

   - **List your happy friends; those who make you feel good** so that when you say goodbye to them you sigh a happy sigh and feel pleased and privileged to know them. Who's got your back?

My Positive Peeps

List the names of the happiest people you know and those who make you feel good, who uplift you and make you FLOURISH and thus make you want to spend more of your time with them:

I WILL SPEND MORE TIME WITH:

This exercise may present you with a dilemma. If you are like most people, you may have a few friends who you have known for a long-time and feel loyal to yet who:

a) aren't very positive people (always complaining, saying negative things about their own lives and the lives of other people);
b) make you feel bad or low after you've spent time with them for whatever reason (they may criticise you or make you feel guilty about having more than them);
c) sap your energy but through no fault of their own. They may just have been through the mill and have had to deal with a lot of negative experiences so they lean on you as a friend. You adore them, but these days all they seem to talk about is themselves and theirproblems.

Some people embarking on a journey to becoming a flourisher would stop seeing all of these people. I would not recommend 'decluttering' all of these people from your life. A friend is a friend after all and you'd hope that, should you experience bad times and need a shoulder to cry on, that your friends would stick around to listen and support you rather than run for the hills because you are sharing your problems, fears and concerns. While we should try not to affect others with our emotional contagion, it is important to talk to other people about anything that is bothering us. A problem shared is a problem halved after all. Talking things through with a good friend can make us feel better, as can helping a friend talk through their problems. And so, my advice would be to maintain contact and continue to be a good friend to those who fit into category 'c'. Even sending an encouraging card or flowers to them as well as seeing them so you can be a good friend to them. That's what friends are for (in part) to listen and accept friends warts and all even when times are hard. I would advise talking to those in category 'b' about how they sometimes make you feel (not in a confrontational way, but just because you want to stay friends so would rather deal with this together rather than stop seeing each other, or see each other less because of it) and, frankly, those who fall in category 'a' could be worth moving on from, unless they are really close and good long-term friends who have been good friends to you (there for you when you needed them) and there is a root cause why are they are not being very nice that you think you can deal with and help them through to change and become a better person. However if they haven't been a good friend to you and are selfish and unkind, it is time to move on, because you deserve better.

Don't feel guilty. This is your one and only life and you deserve to spend time with people who deserve to have you in their lives. Because YOU are lovely and amazing.

There is a dichotomy to this area. On the one hand you should avoid toxic friendships and opt to spend time with feel-good friends. On the other hand you should love people just the way people are, because nobody's perfect. The latter is especially true of actual loved ones (family members/husbands/wives... people who are part of your life). After all the same person can make the morning fabulous and the evening rubbish, depending on their mood.

2. **Compromise, have the moral-high ground and do what is RIGHT and GOOD.** As a flourisher, while truly toxic people should be avoided, you can compromise when it comes to people you don't click as well with or who do something to upset you.

   - **Cherish your gorgeous gaggle of girly friends.** There may be members of your girly group who you don't click with as much as others but no matter. It's just lovely to have a group of friends who you can unwind/de-stress/have fun/laugh/share/rant/express yourself with, so embrace that and them.

   - **Be glad to be you.** When people do things that annoy you, choose to think 'well, I wouldn't do it that way,' or 'what a shame they feel the need to do that.' Better to have that calm feeling of gratitude for being you than to get angry or cross or let someone else's rude or selfish actions bring you down and incite equally rude or selfish actions in yourself. Be better than that. Choose patience. Not always easy but right and good.

3. **Love your loved ones just the way they are.** You cannot force someone you love to change their personality; to do the jobs you want doing, to pay you more compliments, to be more affectionate or less grumpy. The moment you realise this and stop expecting the impossible from them you will begin to feel less animosity and bitterness and, in doing so, in loving him or her just the way they are, you'll generate a more positive vibe and loving atmosphere that will enable your relationship to FLOURISH. The same goes for children. You may wish they didn't have a gruesome obsession with mini-beasts and gore; or prefer that they did as they were told immediately ever single time with no back-chat but, while we can and should discipline and set boundaries/rules and shape our children to a certain extent, (certainly in terms of behaviour) we cannot change

who they are inside. They are amazing and unique. Love them for that. Love them as they are and you'll find an inner patience and appreciation for them, warts and all.

- **Stop over-expecting from your relationships.** A good marriage for example takes work, give and take. There may have been fireworks, passion, butterflies and an intense feeling of love at the start which may have reduced and been replaced with a general feeling of contentment, a warm safe feeling, a security of mutual respect, an admiration. Congratulations. That is brilliant! So many couples go from intensely passionate to intensely resentful for a whole variety of reasons. Partly because they place too much pressure on each other to live up to ridiculously high standards of constant affection, generosity, and passion. Keep it real. If you are content, safe, secure, respectful, and you admire each other – you are one of the lucky ones, so be grateful.

- **Jot down a positive trait of your other half and a positive trait that you have.** Do this on a weekly basis. In order to flourish we need to love ourselves and our partners just as we/they are.

I LOVE US

Here is why:

ME   HIM

- **Write down why you love them warts-and-all.**
  According to studies by Sandra Murray, how you view
  your other half in terms of how clever, good looking,
  funny, loyal, kind and so on in comparison to how your
  closest friends view him/her can reveal how strong your
  relationship is. If your friends view them more highly
  than you do, you have work to do. If you see him/her as
  positively or more positively than your friends do, you
  have a strong relationship.

I love	because
and his/her	is just part of the whole package without which they wouldn't be them.
And I love	just the way he/she is.

REASONS TO GIVE MYSELF A BREAK:
I love MYSELF because I am

- **Accept your differences** You're a team, you and him/
  her. The best and most effective teams have skills and
  characteristics which compliment each others; where
  one person's strengths fill the gaps in another person's
  weaknesses, and vice versa. So, while you may have a
  good deal in common, try to celebrate and appreciate
  your differences too. These are what make you a great
  team. Yes, his perfectionism in the kitchen (the way he
  grumbles vehemently about breaking an egg yolk while
  you really aren't bothered – it's just an egg) may seem
  annoying, but that trait can come in incredibly useful

when it comes to putting something together properly with due care and attention while you scramble something together. Equally, your ability to see the bigger picture and not sweat the small stuff may come in useful when he's getting stressed and needs a calm hand of reason. Look for the bright side in your loved ones, even in the characteristics that annoy you; see how they might be useful. Even his grumpiness after a day at work can be seen in a positive light – far better that he is sharing with you the minutiae of his daily annoyances than keeping it bottled up, painting an unreal picture or lying to you. He's being grumpy, but at least he's being honest, including you and sharing his thoughts with you. So give each other a break. We're all just 'battling through', some of us more than others. Show empathy even if you don't get it back. Let your other half be true to themselves. You want the real authentic version of them, warts and all. If they are messy, so be it. You can nag until you're blue in the face. Tidiness is not in their nature. Get a cleaner. Appreciate that we are different.

- **Encourage independence.** Before you came along your other half did their own thing. Limitations can create resentment. Yes, you may now have responsibilities which need to be shared, such as putting the children to bed. As such, disappearing off to the pub every single night is hardly fair. So compromise. My other half goes fishing quite often on Sundays. Fishing has been his passion since he was eight years old. It makes him incredibly happy, puts him in a good mood and enables him to flourish. How selfish would I be to make him feel guilty about going or insist that he stop. Fishing makes him happy so that makes me happy. Plus I enjoy the one to one time I get with my daughter. We spend a full day on Saturdays together and I relish the times on week nights when he pops round a friend's house because it gives me time all to myself, which I enjoy. Spending time apart is healthy. Living in each others' pockets isn't. Mutual trust furnishes respect which, in turn begets security. Encouraging each other to do what each other loves to do is so important. Support each others' interests outside of each other. Enable each other to flourish separately and together. If you felt hen-pecked and hemmed-in, the desire to escape would be far greater than if you were trusted and supported. Encourage rather than discourage. Respect rather than restrict. In doing so your other half will admire you, appreciate you and stick by you.

- **Be grateful for the little things.** Actions speak louder than words. Don't give your other half a hard time because they fail to shower you with gifts/affection/ praise. They may reveal their admiration, respect and love for you in other ways. They might not be romantic whatsoever. However, they may phone you to ask your opinion on wording for an important e-mail or what they think they should do about a certain situation. They might communicate with you regularly and you may laugh together A LOT. If your other half values and respects your opinion, that in itself reveals that he/ she holds you in admiration, just as the fact that he/ she treats you like a best friend – banter and all. If they are always honest with you, that shows that they care. That's all you should need. If that's the case, but he/ she is not romantic or affectionate, be grateful to have a respectful dignified love and a relationship built on trust and admiration.

- **Try giving your partner whatever it is that you'd like more of from him/her.** First list three things that you'd like more of in your relationship, for example 1) to be listened to and considered 2) to be thanked and praised 3) to get more lie-ins. Before asking your partner to provide you with these things, try giving them to your partner and see what happens. Listen attentively when he/she speaks and ask questions so they can relive what they're telling you about. Offer praise and say 'thank you' more often. Let him/her lie-in and even be 'Queen or King' for the day (not a birthday, just a random day where they get whatever they like). You may find you get the same in return without even asking. (Or not! But you'll be more able to persuade them to provide you with the same if they've experienced how lovely it felt).

- **Forgive your parents.** They most probably did the very best they could. Their best may not have been good enough, but you should still try to forgive. They may have inflicted a lack of love on you. There may have been domestic violence or they might have led you to have limiting belief in yourself that has resulted in a lifelong lack of self-esteem. You may blame them, or one of them, for favouring your sibling, discouraging you from your dreams or stifling your need to express yourself. And yet, the chances are they/he/she tried their best to be a decent parent and acted that way because of a reason they maybe can't be blamed for. Don't see yourself as a victim of them. You didn't live their life or have the same pressures. So accept them and don't blame them. What's done is done.

Ultimately, my mum and my dad brought me into the world. They gave me the most amazing and happy childhood. I was blissfully happy as a child, so completely and utterly loved, valued and encouraged. From the age of 12 I witnessed some major problems at home but, until that point, everything was rosy. I thank them for that. And I'm even thankful for the hard times because they all made me stronger and contributed to make me the person that I am today. My mum and my dad were good parents.

Some life coaches suggest writing a letter to your parents (one which you may never give them, but one which expresses your anger and then forgives them.)

- **Treat your parents with respect.** Avoid sighing, tutting, shaking your head when they talk. Be nice to them. They gave you life. They are your parents. See more of them if possible and listen attentively when they talk. They will not be around forever and you WILL miss them when they are gone – more than you even realise. You will wish you could phone them just one more time and listen to them wittering on. But you won't be able to because they've gone. So make the most of your time with your parents while they are still around.

This may contradict what has previously been said about decluttering negative/toxic people. If your parent(s) constantly criticise you or are negative people, seeing more of them will not enable you to flourish. That said, phoning them more frequently, posting a magazine they might like to read, doing something kind while keeping your distance but still swallowing your pride/anger and making time to see them on occasions is important.

Commit to Spend More Time With Other People

"Of all the things that wisdom provides for living one's entire life in happiness, the greatest by far is the possession of friendship,"
Epicurus

Familiarity breeds affection. With other people contributing so much to our well-being, a commitment to spend more time with them is a vital ingredient to flourish. Relationships require effort to sustain them and keep them strong.

On a slightly morbid but worthy note, in her book *The Top Five Regrets of the Dying*, Palliative care nurse, Bronnie Ware, says a top regret is not having stayed in touch with friends.

"Often they would not truly realise the full benefits of old friends until their dying weeks and it was not always possible to track them down. Many had become so caught up in their own lives that they had let golden friendships slip by over the years. There were many deep regrets about not giving friendships the time and effort that they deserved."

4. **Devote more time to your positive relationships with family and friends**. Relationships will only last if you put in the effort consistently to maintain them. And, while good friends understand that busy lives mean they have to pick up where they left off and may not see you for a month or so, that doesn't mean you should relax and ignore each other completely.

   Make time, not only because seeing people you love makes you and them feel good but also to repay them for loving you. Reward them with your time. Remember, connecting with others, especially those we enjoy spending time with, boosts happiness and enables us to flourish.

   • **Strengthen old friendships and touch base.** Make a note to contact friends from your past who remind you of 'home' or who remind you of you as a happy and flourishing child. I have three friends who I only see once a year or so, but, every time I see Karen, Helen or Lisa I feel a burst of overwhelming joy. They remind me of a pre-teen innocent and blissfully happy me; they knew my mum really well; (pretty much all of my friends who I see regularly sadly never got to meet her) they are dear to me and I to them. I love to see them. I should therefore try to make time to see them more often than once a year. But I am glad that I see them at least that much. Life without those friends wouldn't be the same. They connect me to a happy past and make me feel at home, secure and loved.

Arrange to meet old friends once or twice each year at the very least. Message them and get something in the diary for term breaks/holidays. Send an e-newsletter to old friends at Christmas or New Year and again on their birthday (to go with their card).

- **Deepen existing friendships.** Take some one-to-one time with your favourite individuals from your group of friends; book an annual holiday or spa break that you all go on together.

- **Schedule social contact into your daily routine.** Make time for your relationships. Schedule it in literally. Because, if you don't, you won't see them. Whether that's sending a FB message, making a phonecall, skyping, texting or meeting up for a coffee – put it in the diary. Life gets in the way and, while true friends understand and appreciate that we may have to postpone get-togethers or are too busy this week to speak or see each other; in order to flourish we need to find the time to have that social contact, even if it's a quick phone call in between lunch and work; but ideally find the time to plan a spa weekend or pub lunch or woodland walk together.

In your weekly planner include a block of time (mine is on Sunday evenings just before or after teatime) when you text or message friends in some way to book in some time to see each other or mention something that's been niggling you or just have a chat. Schedule in a regular meet-up of existing friendships (eg Wednesday girly night) where you meet up weekly or monthly at the very least at each other's houses.

- **Schedule to do more together as a family too.** Whether that is playing golf, badminton or tennis, going for regular walks, going to the park, finger-painting, kite-flying or playing Scrabble, cards or chess. Create a routine in which you do at least one of those things together every week. It's all too easy just to sit and watch telly together. Interact more. Even do your chores or declutter together. After Christmas, my daughter, husband and I, like most households, spend a day together taking down the decorations. We also de-cluttered the house. We took bags and boxes of stuff to the dump then popped into the supermarket together to get a special treat for tea. Teamwork and teamplay, especially of the family-kind, boosts positive emotions and strengthens relationships.

Ask your other half what they really love to do, then schedule in some of that feel-good stuff into your family flourish planner. See Chapter 5 for FLOURISH ACTIVITIES.

LET'S HAVE FLOURISHING FUN TOGETHER

My other half loves to:

- ○
- ○
- ○
- ○
- ○
- ○

- **Provide support to your friends.** Being supportive is proven to boost happiness more than being supported. Good deeds beget good feelings. Making others happy makes you happy. Being generous with the time and effort you invest in being a supportive friend is far more satisfying for you and your friends than showering them with expensive gifts.

How can you help your friends out? How can you encourage them to follow their dreams? How can you introduce them to someone who can help them; to other sources of support that they didn't yet have? Can you organise reunions? Can you introduce them to this handbook and work on it together, so that you can both flourish? Can you spend an evening or two creating photo CDs for friends which include all the photos you have of them and their children? If your friend is launching a new business, scrap your plans and attend the launch for moral support. If they have had a baby, book in time to see them as soon as they are ready. If you are too busy to see someone, send a thoughtful card.

I'm a Good Friend

List the ways you can support your friends better here. I will provide more support to my friends by:

○

○

- **Consider ways to make new friends.** Brand new friendships introduce you to new interests, people, opportunities and activities and expand your world. Join a local club to find people with shared interests. Arrange a get together among the school mums of children in your child's class; include those you don't yet speak to. Attend local events and fitness classes. Get yourself out there. Mingle.

Consider How You Communicate
With Other People

What we say and how we say it can directly affect the well-being of other people. So, about that...

- **Be nicer to each other.** We are often way more critical of our other half than we are of our best friend (or even strangers). There is a polite way to speak to others, but it seems to be fine to belittle or criticise our family members and partners. Why is that? Oddly it is a fact that most of us show more consideration for our friends/strangers than we do our husbands or wives. We give others the benefit of the doubt and judge less harshly. And yet it our other half who is our soul mate, our complete and utter best friend, the love of our life. So be nice to each other. We are often more courteous and nicer to complete strangers, colleagues and friends than we are to our other halves and yet your chosen other half is your "one in seven billion." Furthermore, the vibe and atmosphere of your relationship dictates how you feel and act each day. Bickering in the morning can create a downcast forecast, while jovial banter and praise results in a glorious forecast and a day filled with sunshine. Devote time to consider how you might behave differently to create a better weather forecast for your relationships. Could you do something yourself rather than nag him/her to do it? Could you give him/her the benefit of the doubt more often? Give each other a break! You're a team.

  Patience and praise are two of the most vital ingredients in a healthy relationship. Listen and nurture rather than nag and neglect.

  You have the power to make someone else feel incredibly happy or sad. In fact, in having chosen to spend the rest of your days together, you are devoting your life to their happiness, to making them happy. That's a big responsibility. But one that can be made far easier if you are simply nice to them.

- **Show empathy.** Be helpful. Put yourself in other people's shoes. Try to see something from their point of view. So what that you are not shown the same courtesy. They are not flourishing, you are, so bring the win-win attitude to relationships. By considering what's in it for the other person, you can create a mutually-beneficial situation. Seeing things from other people's perspectives, having empathy enables stronger relationships and better decision-making. You will make choices based on mutual benefit and be able to better negotiate with business partners, work colleagues, spouses, siblings and children to create situations that everyone is happy with. Hurrah!

- **Stop complaining.** It's draining. While other people like to give advice or help and it can make you feel better if you have a rant, (yes a problem shared is a problem halved) dumping your negative energy onto others and out into the universe can actually multiply the negative feeling you feel about something and drag others down. Remember emotional contagion? Avoid spreading negativity. If something is troubling you discuss it with your close confidantes but in a positive 'let's find a solution' kind of way, rather than a 'doom and gloom' manner. Try out the phrases 'never mind', 'oh well,' 'c'est la vie'. Don't let the minutiae of life drag you (and others around you) down. Stride boldly over obstacles and smile.

- **Be up around people you love.** Be cheerful. Stay positive. Don't complain, moan, grumble. Respond with, 'really well, thank you' rather than 'not bad' when people ask how you are. By lifting your own spirits you'll notice that you have the power to life other people's. Emotional contagion works the other way too. :-)

- **Praise and pay compliments.** Encourage and congratulate people for doing something well. Comment on a lovely jumper or on a colour suiting someone. Be genuine.

- **Focus on the positive rather than the negative.** The Losada ratio, named after Marcel Losada, is a rule that applies to all relationships. In order to flourish you need to **give five positive statements for every critical statement.** Barbara Fredrickson used this ratio to study companies during business meetings, transcribing every single word said to support her belief that the positive/negative statement ratio tied in with how much the companies were economically flourishing. Her assumptions were correct. Try to top focusing on what your other half has done wrong instead of what he or she has done right. Switch your focus onto what they are doing right and well. Praise instead of criticise, encourage instead of nag. If you need to draw attention to something that needs doing, gentle genuine praise first will work more effectively than ploughing straight into a critical nag. Just as you should stop focusing on correcting other peoples' weaknesses instead of building their strengths, you should stop focusing on your own shortcomings and concentrate on what makes you brilliantly you – your strengths... as we saw in Chapter 4.

- **Show an interest in what other's say to you.** Listen intently rather than being preoccupied with other things or merely waiting for your opportunity to express your view point. Say encouraging things to show you're listening, such as 'I see what you mean,' and 'you're absolutely right'.

- **Respond better. Respond constructively.** There are different ways of responding when our friends and loved ones tell us about a good day or triumph they've experienced. Avoid raining on people's parade, no matter what your opinion is.

1. Constructive responses where you not only praise the person for their achievement but also show an interest by asking them to relive the experience, strengthens the relationship. For example: "That's great news, I'm really proud of you. So tell me more about what happened... what did he say? Then what? And how did you react? Nice one. Let's celebrate. You deserve it."

2. De-constructive responses undermine and weaken relationships. For example: "That sounds to me like you're going to be away from home even more than you are now? Do you think you can honestly manage that?"

There are non-verbal ways of communicating to encourage or discourage too. If you smile, laugh, touch and retain eye contact, you are actively encouraging someone and showing interest. Conversely if you walk away when being spoken to or show no emotion or expression, you are being passive (and rude). We lead busy lives and we all are guilty of occasionally questioning some good news or being inpatient when someone is trying to share something with us. But that doesn't strengthen relationships and positive relationships are mutually good for everyone's well-being. The more you respond constructively and actively to people; the more you ask people to tell you more and relive details of something good that they are sharing with you, the more people will want to spend time with you and share with you; and the better you will feel about yourself as a friend and good listener. Communicating constructively is a win-win.

Exercise:

Practice being a better friend or 'other half' by responding actively and constructively to those who share a positive experience with you. Show your support enthusiastically, be authentic in your interest and ask who, what, where, when, why and how questions so that they flesh out the details and tell you, for instance, what the new job is, what they'll be doing, how they felt when they got the news, what they're most looking forward to about it and so on. Avoid merely commenting, 'nice one' or worse, ignoring the good news completely and shifting the conversation over to be all about you, or asking negative questions such as, 'won't the hours/travel/childcare be more of a problem to manage?'

Notice when you found it easiest and most difficult to respond constructively. Maybe feeling tired prevented you from caring enough to ask questions? Maybe your own exciting news overshadowed someone else's? Learn to make more of an effort during those instances.

- **Be genuinely happy for others when they share their good news.** Back-handed compliments which make people feel guilty for having more/doing well. e.g. 'you're so lucky to have this that or the other... I wish I did; we can hardly afford to blah blah blah' make the other person feel guilty, even though they have no reason to feel bad. It is not their fault that they have what they have.

  When someone tells you their good news about a promotion or holiday plans or having done something exciting, be pleased for them, ask them to relive it for you, ask questions.

- **Say sorry first whenever possible.** Clear the air. This doesn't mean you are admitting that you were wrong and they were right. Say sorry for arguing, which you have both done, so apologise for having an argument and move on with tension diffused.

- **Be impressive. Go the extra mile from time to time.** Who do you love more than anyone else in the whole entire world? Your loved ones are your loved ones because, um, yes, you LOVE THEM. So demonstrate that by going the extra mile from time to time. Make their birthday treat exceed their expectations, plan a special treat or weekend away. Delight your other half with a little surprise here and there. Buy them a present for no reason other than to say you love them (not on Valentines Day or Birthday or Father's Day... just on a Tuesday in any normal week).

- **Become a more patient, peaceful and playful parent.** As mums and dads leading increasingly busy lives, being patient, remaining calm and finding time to play isn't always easy. However, this is your child's actual childhood. Right now. And it won't last long. Nope, they won't be small for much longer. Enjoy your children by resolving to be more patient, peaceful and playful. Here's a few ideas how to do that:

  o In the moment, when your child asks you to build a den with them or read them a story AGAIN for the umpteenth time, let go of the 'don't have time' response and try not to do it begrudgingly. Pretend you're five again and try to enjoy it.
  o Nip whining in the bud by singing a silly distracting response or writing down your child's grievance. You can also try this approach: Say 'I wish I had a magic wand. If I did I'd [insert grievance here] e.g. make it stop raining so you could go to the park'.
  o Show that you're listening and that you understand by showing empathy. When your child starts to cry because they couldn't do something or they

wanted something acknowledge those feelings by telling them how you think they're feeling. For example 'You're feeling sad and frustrated because you couldn't do such and such. I know. Mummy feels like that sometime when I can't find my keys. So here's what we'll do.... (See *How To Talk So Your Kids Will Listen* book, which includes loads more advice like this.)

o Go to the park early on summer mornings before breakfast on occasion as a special treat.

o Be loving rather than argumentative wherever possible. Take a deep breath or walk away if you feel like you are about to get angry. Say you are not going to argue if your child is answering back, walk away and count slowly to ten.

o Replace 'no', 'don't' and 'stop' with 'Hey! Let's do this instead' or 'Yes once we have done such as such we can do such and such'.

o Be silly. It uplifts those around you. It's that "emotional contagion" effect. Yay! Burp! Oops! Giggle :-)

o Let your children make mistakes. They will have friends you don't like. They will make mistakes, but they need that freedom to make mistakes in order to learn properly, not just from you telling them, but for real. To learn important lessons in life. Too much protection can be detrimental in later life if they've made no mistakes of their own and been wrapped in cotton wool. Let them experience life and learn.

o Let them help from time to time. "Can I help?" asks your child when you are cooking tea or doing something when you would much rather have them sitting quietly in the lounge while you concentrate on the task at hand and have some much-needed me-time. You'd rather not indulge them because you know they will say "mummy" at least 84 times within the next 10 minutes. However, "of course my darling," is how you should respond and you will make their day. And our children's happiness is our core aim in life isn't it? And seeing them happy makes us happy doesn't it? So try it sometimes. It may be messier, it may take longer, but it's worth it to see that proud smile on their little squishy faces.

- Be calm. Shout less. I always ALWAYS feel bad after shouting. It doesn't help me to release any pent up aggression. It merely makes me feel rubbish. Also, when my daughter subsequently shouts back at me, I feel even worse as that is 100% my fault. I have taught her to do that. She has modelled that behaviour entirely on her mother's lack of control. I need to instead demonstrate better self-control and more patience, just as my own mother did. This may involve counting to 10 (almost always works), reciting a poem (I like A.A.Milne's *"James James Morrison Morrison Weatherby George Dupree took great care of his mother, though he was only three"*, leaving the room, taking a deep breath, swallowing pride. Indeed, when I do respond calmly but firmly to events that I might otherwise ordinarily have shouted in response to, it works. The outcome is always way better than that induced from a shouting match. Stuff gets done. We stay friends. All is well.

- Give yourself a break. We all have moments when we shout or impatiently get annoyed with our children and generally think we are rubbish mummies for whatever reason (see above). The likelihood is that you are a totally BRILLIANT MUMMY who shows love, compassion to your child and do all you can to keep him/her/them safe and happy. It's not easy. Every mum everywhere has moments we wish we could have responded differently. That's just the way it is. Don't beat yourself up about it. Remember, it's going to be OK. You have got a good 18 years or so to transform your little pickle from a mud-hurling, squabbling, whiny, shouty, frowny, naughty little pickle into a polite, thoughtful, kind and happy, respectable grown-up. Phew!

Behave Well: Flourisher Social Behaviour Is Kind, Patient And True

It has been scientifically proven that carrying out acts of kindness boosts well-being more than any other method/exercise/practice/action. It's a mutual serotonin-raiser.

- **Scatter kindness on a regular (daily or weekly) basis.** Go on. Go and do something that will positively affect someone else's happiness and well-being. Do a good deed today or tomorrow and you'll feel truly great. This in turn will provide these days with meaning and engagement, thus ticking those two flourishing boxes AND will provide you with with positive emotion as a result. Help someone out. Notice how your mood is lifted when you do so. If you continue to do this, notice the effect on your well-being.

- **List ways you can be continually kind**, whether its supporting a good cause, volunteering your time, leaving change when paying for goods, passing on a parking ticket to someone else (not the kind you get from a traffic warden but the kind you get to enable you to park, obviously)... let someone in front of you, bake a cake or cook a meal and give it to someone who needs it; help a mum carrying a pushchair, give your seat up for someone, give someone advice or help to achieve a goal you know they're passionate about. Share advice, goods, food, services, advice, recommendations... You could even share this link: www.flourishhandbook.com with your friends to equip them with the means to boost their well-being and give yourself a well-being boost knowing that you might be improving someone's life. Doing something nice for someone creates a very high feel good factor in you and the chosen recipient. Spread the love lovely.

- **List people you can be kind to and how so.** For example, your friend may be having trouble finding a job; or may benefit from a brainstorming session to help her find her true purpose; or perhaps you are knowledgeable about a topic that will be of use to a friend or family member. Perhaps they need help setting up a profile on LinkedIn or could do with some company when their other half is away.

MY BE KIND TO DO LIST

This week/month I shall scatter kindness by:
-
-
-

Schedule these good deeds into your Flourish Planner

- **Emulate kind people.** Who is the kindest person you know? Who is the most positive person you know? How about the most patient person? Can you try to emulate their kindness/ positivity/patience and ask them about how they sustain that? Model their behaviour, use them as positive role models. This shouldn't make you feel bad because you are not as positive or patient as them; your aim here is to improve your positivity and patience; that's a good thing to be doing.

To Do List and Planner

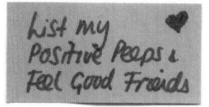

List my Positive Peeps & Feel Good Friends ♥

Write letter of forgiveness

Check diary & Book TIMES to SEE FRIENDS ♥

FLOURISH PLANNER (ongoing)

Schedule in:
- A block of time to make calls/send text messages/e-mails to those listed in my My Positive Peeps list and book in time to see them this week/month/year. Make it happen. Make my friendships flourish!
- A block of time to lend support to friends
- Regular meet ups of existing friends
- New friend get-togethers / classes to meet new people
- Daily noting down of positive traits of me and him/her in the 'I Love Us' worksheet.
- Fun activities that my other half/kids love to do, including more 'play' time.
- Time to do good deeds/acts of kindness.

Printable Quotes... to cut out n stick up

"A friend is someone who gives you total freedom to be yourself."

Jim Morrison

"My best friend is the one who brings out the best in me."

Henry Ford

"Let us be grateful to people who make us happy, they are the charming gardeners who make our souls blossom."

Marcel Proust

"The only way to have a friend is to be one."

Ralph Waldo Emerson

Part 4

Growth and Achievement

Chapter 8

MONTH EIGHT: Sustaining an Attitude of Gratitude

"What a wonderful life I've had. I only wish I'd realised it sooner,"
Colette

Enjoying Now And What You Already Have

Despite having so much more opportunity, more stuff and more potential to flourish, society as a whole is reportedly less happy than it used to be. A major cause of this downward spiral is due to a modern-day default focus on lack, coupled with increasingly higher expectations. We expect more and thus feel inadequate when our excessive expectations are not met. And that feeling of lacking wealth or health creates more sadness than being wealthy or healthy creates happiness. Sad but true.

If modern society could focus on celebrating what we DO have instead of what we DON'T, we could, as entire nations, be happier. And, not just happier. It is widely accepted in positive psychology and scientific studies that those who habitually feel and articulate gratitude perform better, sleep better and see health and relationship improvements. It's good to be thankful.

Media has always had a lot to answer for, with its glossy unattainable and air-brushed representations of reality. These days Facebook has a lot to answer for too. While the phenomenal social network can be attributed to many positive well-being inducing effects (enabling enhanced connection, boosting social relationships, offering opportunities to gain support from peers and reminisce in unison through the sharing of personal media, for example) it also intensifies the human nature of comparing our selves and what we have to others and can make us feel inadequate in comparison to our Facebook friends. According to research, as human beings we measure ourselves in relation to other people. We compare ourselves and our lives/accomplishments to other people who are either better off or worse off. Most of us focus on those who are better off; those who have a better house, nicer garden and are better looking... or those who have something that we want but don't yet have, whether that's a home of our own, a partner, a child. This daily reminder of what we long for but don't have can deflate us. While comparison among peers tends to lead to dissatisfaction; we can use this default assessment to our advantage. We can use the comparisons to those better off to spur us on to achieve what we want and comparisons with those worse off to consider what we should be more grateful for; what we should stop taking for granted; what we should take time to APPRECIATE!

Because... guess what?

Your happiness is right here, under your nose, under your own roof, right here, right now! Of course, you could spend your life seeking it and striving to achieve it and, while there are changes you can make, goals you can pursue and exercises you can do to boost your well-being, much of it is actually ALREADY HERE if you just know where to look. So, before you start formulating your future to bring your desired dreams of your ideal destiny to fruition, LOOK UNDER YOUR OWN ROOF; seek happiness in the here and now, examine what you already have to be grateful for, because there is always, ALWAYS something to be grateful for today! Focusing on what you DO have, rather than what you DON'T have is a powerful attractor. As Oprah Winfrey points out:

"Be thankful for what you have; you'll end up having more.
If you concentrate on what you don't have,
you will never, ever have enough"
Oprah Winfrey

Being grateful attracts more to be grateful about. Numerous studies reveal that an "attitude of gratitude" makes people happier and healthier by attracting more of what they want and boosts well-being immensely. The University of California measured health and well-being in a study of students who thought about five things they were grateful for on a daily basis. They showed increased joyfulness and improved health issues compared to those who didn't do this regular exercise of appreciation.

If you focus your thoughts and actions on what you don't have (e.g. worrying about not having enough money) then you'll attract more of the same (not enough money). Conversely if you appreciate what you do have and what you believe you will have soon (as if you already have it) you will attract more of that good stuff into your life, that's what you'll attract. According to the Law of Attraction, the Universe doesn't know the difference between past, present and future. It is responding to your current feeling and delivering you more of the same. Counting your blessings is the quickest way to get yourself out of a grump too! Furthermore, gratitude reduces feelings of envy and inadequacy.

In order to truly flourish you need to work on feeling great and appreciating what you have right NOW, without having pots of cash to spend at your every whim. Feel happy and grateful and on top of the world WITHOUT money. The alternative is to constantly feel that you can't afford this or that you need more money. If that feeling and though-process is a constant in your life, that's what you'll attract and you'll always need more money and will never afford what you want. So move your thought-process away from that need. Feel happier now with what you already have and stop constantly thinking that you need more. It's not easy, but this very handbook will give you tools and exercises and methods to help you to do that.

> *"One of the most tragic things I know about human nature is that all of us tend to put off living. We are all dreaming of some magical rose garden over the horizon - instead of enjoying the roses blooming outside our windows today,"*
> **Dale Carnegie**

So, appreciate what you already have. Appreciate the version of you that is living and breathing NOW, today. I bet you wish you had appreciated the 21 year old version of you more when you were 21, right? Instead of wistfully waiting for your desired destiny? Oh how time flies. So enjoy who you are, what you do, who you are with. Relish your reality, cherish the choices you have made to make you YOU. This you. The you who is reading these words on this day in time RIGHT NOW.

If you are doing something you love. Have people you love, who love you; if you are doing what you love and love what you do. That's the fun part, that's the reward. Sit back and ENJOY THAT. Relish the joy of happiness that TODAY brings because of that. Cherish how lucky you are. Do this every day. Feel that gratitude and smile! Conversely if your weight, job, singleton status or something else is dragging you down... feel grateful for what you DO have: your health, your family, your senses; appreciate your life – it is wonderful to be alive; regardless of the anxieties, worries, fears, sadness – you still have *something* to be grateful for. As Robert Fulghum wisely says: "If you break your neck, if you have nothing to eat, if your house is on fire, then you've got a problem. Everything else is inconvenience." So, get grateful. Then tackle the areas that are pulling you down, one-by-one, step-by-step, knowing and believing that you're OK. Because you are. Being grateful for what you already have, for the you that already exists, is the first step to ensuring that.

Evidently, if you can schedule in 'thankfulness' time and undertake some activities that **focus on gratitude,** you can not only feel better about your life as it presently exists and enjoy your life more (and boost your well-being in the process) you can also attract the things you wish you already had too. A ginormous win-win.

Harnessing And Practising
A Powerful Attitude Of Gratitude

Gratitude can be felt, expressed and recorded. Aim to do all three. Here's how:

1. **Cherish now more.** Enjoy this present moment in time, this day. Truly appreciate everything that you have right now. Don't wait for your desired future to bring you happiness. Instead of always thinking, "I'll be happy when I get that job/house/car/have children/get married" think I'm happy now and here's why. This "I'll be happy when" belief that achieving a certain goal will make you happy is known as the "arrival fallacy" in Tal Ben-Shahar's book, *Happier*. As we'll examine in Chapter 10, achieving that happiness-inducing goal tends not to live up to those expectations as much as you think it will. By the time you are achieving your goal, you're already experiencing it, so it's already been absorbed into your overall sense of well-being. Furthermore there may be other emotions that come with you arriving at your desired destination. When you have a baby there's worry/fear/insecurity alongside intense happiness.

Meanwhile the seeds of fresh goals are planted as soon as you reach that one you were so sure would make everything so wonderful.

So what's a flourisher to do?

The key is to enjoy making *progress* towards a dream; enjoy the *actual JOURNEY*! Relish the process and your progress in the present.

There are a variety of ways to do this in order to appreciate and savour what is going well in your life TODAY. Here is how to enjoy the joy in NOW:

- **Keep a gratitude diary/journal.** Stop focusing on what went wrong today or in your past and focus instead of what went right! Sure, we should assess our mistakes to avoid repeating them, but dwelling on negative stuff is not helpful. At the end of every day before bed (or every other day, so that you do this at least three-four times per week) devote 10-15 minutes to this exercise. So what kinds of stuff might you feel grateful for? For being able to see, hear, speak, feel, touch? For being alive and breathing right now, and now, and now. (Just ask anyone with a terminal illness). For having a roof over your head and a bed to sleep in, for hot water, clothes and food; for your job/career/work and the experiences and opportunities they provide you with; for your friends, for your family, for being able to get what you need thanks to local shops and the internet, for knowledge and insight that you gain from books, magazines, TV/radio and other mediums; for being able to read; for the sun, for the rain, for nature. Just. Thank you.

  - **Record your gratitude**. This is a great daily habit to get into.
    - Write down five general blessings that you are grateful for. These are your gratitude statements. For example: "Today I am truly thankful for my healthy daughter, the good health of myself and my other half, living in this beautiful village, working from home, doing my dream job."

    - Now note down three good things that happened to you today for which you are grateful, plus why they happened and/or what this means to you. "I received an encouraging text – this happened because I sent an encouraging text first. My daughter told me she loved me – this happened because I stopped to hug her. Our shopping was delivered – this means I can spend more quality play time with my daughter after school instead of taking her shopping with me."

- Be thankful for tomorrow as well as today. As you lay down to go to sleep, give thanks for all the amazing things that you want to happen the following day, as if that day too has passed. Repeat this process in the morning, when you wake up. Express and feel gratitude for all that you wish to happen today as if it's already happened.

- **Record moments of happiness.** Consider what moment made you feel happy today? Describe it. e.g. Today on the train home, I spotted two deer on a grassy hill. I felt lucky to have spotted them. That journey also made me recall the joy of a previous train ride home from Chichester after I first met my heroine Dame Anita Roddick (and subsequent visits to see her). I was buzzing with joy and gratitude and how much great stuff has happened since then.

Have a practice run. Start today, start right now, here:

Thank you so much!

I AM BLESSED. Today – I am so TRULY GRATEFUL FOR

1. _____

2. _____

3. _____

4. _____

5. _____

These are my blessings

Thank you for TODAY.   This happened because /

Thank you especially for: this means:

e.g._____   _____

_____   _____

_____   _____

_____   _____

_____   _____

- **Consider whether you could thank anyone in particular for any of those things.** If there is someone specific to thank, call or email them to express your appreciation and thanks. If not, thank the universe or yourself :-)

- **Express thanks to others in general.** Make a concerted effort to look people directly in the eyes and thank them. Just say thank you more. We take so much for granted. Be mindful of this. Part of Martin Seligman's work on flourishing includes what he calls, 'the gratitude visit' – an exercise created by Marisa Lascher. This involves writing a letter of thanks to someone who has helped you in the past and visiting them to read it out loud. It should contain 300 words and specifically focus on what they have done for you and how it has positively impacted your life. After reading it to them Martin suggests that you "discuss the content and your feelings for each other. You will be happier and less depressed one month from now." Gratitude, recognition, acknowledgement and praise are a powerful combination.

- **Feel that gratitude as well as writing it down**. Read out what you are grateful for and turn up the volume on your emotion. Close your eyes and feel that gratitude seeping through you; feel your heart beating with appreciation for what you have. If you are out and about and affirming your gratitude statements, shout (or whisper) them (depending on whether you are alone in a field or in a public place) towards the sky and feel that emotion of appreciation. I have done this in the car and during a walk and have felt so overwhelmed with emotion that I have been close to tears (or have actually sobbed a little bit). That's powerful.

- **Keep a gratitude jar.** In addition to or instead of writing gratitude statements expressing thanks for specific moments or things; write them on a scrap of paper in one-sentence, either as they happen or at the end of each day and pop them in a jar. This will allow you to capture fleeting moments that will soon pass and disappear from your memory. For example, 'Brooke shone today in her drumming concert. So grateful to have her. So happy to work from home so that I get the opportunity to see her shine.' Or 'We made pancakes for breakfast and tea, such a joy to see the excitement in her eyes and the smile on her face.'

- **Create a gratitude board to display on your wall.** (This makes an ideal wall partner for your vision board and should fit snugly next to it − see Chapter Nine). Gather photographs, pictures, words that provide a snapshot of moments, things, people, experiences you are grateful for.

  - **Schedule a gratitude morning on a weekly, monthly or quarterly basis.** Reflect on all that you DO have rather than what you DON'T have. Look back at your daily gratitude diary and feel gratitude for everything you have been thankful for. Devote this morning to focusing on the good positive stuff; on luck not lack. Grab your gratitude jar and have a sift through all the wonderful things that have happened so far. Take time to feel grateful for them.

  - **Review earlier diaries/journals/vision boards/ notebooks which have recorded your desired future in some way.** You will likely discover that you got what you desired. For instance, I recently found a notebook I wrote in 2003, before I had even considered writing a book. I was a freelance writer, editor and business woman. It affirmed the following:
    - o I have met Anita Roddick and Madonna.
    - o I am a best-selling author.
    - o I have a healthy baby daughter.

In 2005 I met Anita Roddick and she kindly agreed to write the Foreword to my book. I haven't yet met Madonna (can't have it all). That book, *The Small Business Start-Up Workbook*, became a best-seller, topping the Start-Up category charts on Amazon and has sold consistently well since it was first published. In 2008 I gave birth to my healthy baby daughter.

Today I am so incredibly grateful for all that I have as I once hoped for it and now I have it. I go on a "gratitude walk" most mornings - a great way to mix exercise and fresh air with giving thanks for what I currently have. It's such an empowering way to start each day.

"Do not spoil what you have by desiring what you have not;
but remember that what you now have was once among the
things you only hoped for."
Epicurus

- **Go on regular gratitude walks. Find a place to go to affirm your gratitude statements and thank the Universe for all that you already have.** Aim to find a place that is quiet and frequented by few people. A place you can call your own. For instance, I have 'our field' – a beautiful field just past the church yard and allotments. Whenever I go there alone, it is usually just me. Occasionally I will see one other dog walker, but usually nobody. We go as a family too. Look up to the sky and thank the universe for all that you have. Add on one or two things that you wish to have, but don't yet have *as if you already DO have them* (more on this later). Say your affirmations out loud and express heartfelt gratitude for each and every thing. As I walk through the field I affirm what I have which I am truly grateful for and what I wish to have and I feel how I might feel if I already had that. So "thank you for my healthy daughter and for all our good health; thank you for this place; thank you that we can now afford to buy our own home; thank you for giving us the opportunity to love what we do for a living and enjoy our work so much; thank you for rewarding us for all our hard work; we are now financially secure, healthy and happy. Thank you!"

"Sometimes you will never know the true value
of a moment until it becomes a memory."
Unknown

My Achievements

Yay! I am proud of me because:

_____

_____

_____

_____

_____

_____

_____

_____

_____

- **Appreciate what you have already achieved.** List your achievements as far back as you can. e.g. A medal for netball when you were 10? 400m cup winner? Sponsored swim? Being made a sixer at Brownies or a prefect at school? Getting THAT job? Having the guts to leave THAT job when you started your own business? Having the guts to leave THAT man when he turned into an arse? Getting an award for something? Helping to nurture your child so that she/he won an award for something?

2. **Cherish and capture precious moments.** You *know* how fast time flies; how quickly children go from being tiny dependent babies to big independent school children. Each precious moment is there one minute and gone the next. If you have a little girl or boy ENJOY your precious time with them. It's oh so easy to reach for that book or catch up on chores or make a phonecall to a friend while your child plays happily. Your instinct as a busy mum is to seize the opportunity while they are occupied to do something you need to do. Sometimes you have no choice. But, sometimes, ignore the dishes/phone your friend in the evening/leave the book until later – avoid distractions, and avoid wasting that precious moment. Instead:

   - **Focus intently on that fleeting moment with your daughter as a little girl; your son as a little boy.** Because, as the poem below iterates, their 'childhood is not here to stay,' they won't be small for very long. This is it - their childhood – right now. So enjoy as much as you can of it, see things through their little eyes, because their childhood is gone before you know it.

   - **Capture those precious moments.** Do so either on film via photo/video and/or in your gratitude diary/journal/jar. Those precious moments will gloriously enable you to flourish as you reminisce on them at a later date.

Gone, but still remembered; captured for you to treasure forever.

Slow down mummy, there is no need to rush,
slow down mummy, what is all the fuss?
Slow down mummy, make yourself a cup of tea.
Slow down mummy, come and spend some time with me.

Slow down mummy, let's put our boots on and go out for a walk,
let's kick at piles of leaves, and smile and laugh and talk.
Slow down mummy, you look ever so tired,
come sit and snuggle under the duvet and rest with me a while.

Slow down mummy, those dirty dishes can wait,
slow down mummy, lets have some fun, lets bake a cake!
Slow down mummy I know you work a lot,
but sometimes mummy, its nice when you just stop.

Sit with us a minute,
& listen to our day,
spend a cherished moment,
because our childhood is not here to stay!

- **Go and look at your children.** If he/she/they are asleep, go and look at them close-up (without waking them) and feel intense gratitude that they exist, that you made them. Or, if they are at school right now or elsewhere, gaze at a happy photo of them and feel thankful. If you don't have children and want to; affirm gratitude statements that you do have them and believe. Your time will come. And appreciate the peace and quiet, the opportunity to lie-in; the freedom to go where you wish at any time and all of the things that having a child can restrict. Enjoy *those* moments. Remember, there is always something to be grateful for.

*"To be without some of the things you want is
an indispensable part of happiness"*

TO DO LIST AND PLANNER

Buy
- Snazzy Notebook & pen
- Jar
- Card for collage

- Keep camera charged and ready

Take PHOTOS + VIDEOS

Go find "my place"

Make a GRATITUDE Board/Collage

FLOURISH PLANNER (ongoing)

Schedule in:
- Time each day to record your gratitude in your gratitude diary/journal or jar
- Daily, weekly or monthly affirmation/gratitude walks in 'your place'.
- Chores/calls/me-time AFTER the child(ren) are in bed, giving you more time to enjoy their childhood with them.

Printable Quotes... to cut out n stick up

"Never let

the things you WANT

make you forget

the things you HAVE."

Jean Vanier

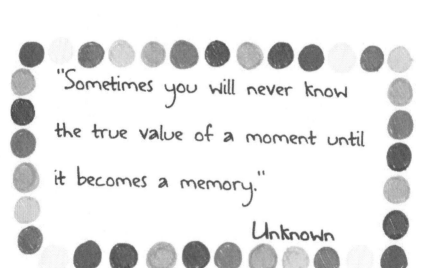

"Sometimes you will never know

the true value of a moment until

it becomes a memory."

Unknown

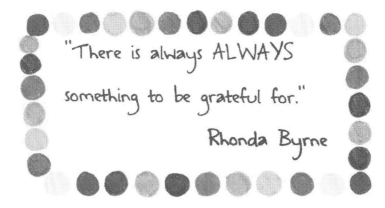

"There is always ALWAYS
something to be grateful for."
Rhonda Byrne

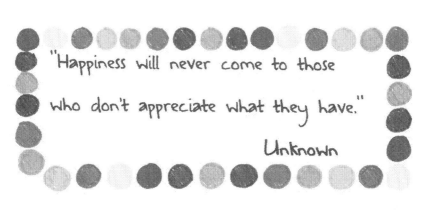

"Happiness will never come to those
who don't appreciate what they have."
Unknown

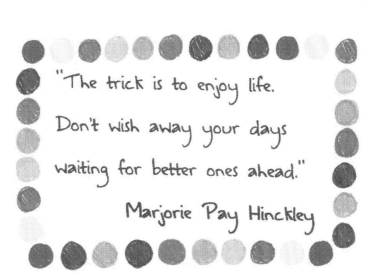

"The trick is to enjoy life.
Don't wish away your days
waiting for better ones ahead."
Marjorie Pay Hinckley

Chapter 9

MONTH NINE:
Create a Vision and
Set Clear Goals

*"The grand essentials to happiness in this life are
something to do, something to love, and something to hope for,"*
Joseph Addison

Defining Your Vision:
What You Wish To Have

So, what is it that you want from this one precious life of yours?
Precisely what do you wish to achieve and accomplish?

You may have specific great big ambitions. You might like to write
a novel or children's book, run a marathon, fly a plane? These
are 'bucket list' type goals and tackling and accomplishing them
provides substantial satisfaction. You may dream of owning your
own 4 bedroom detached home, emigrating to Australia, running
a successful business which employs people, achieving work-life
balance so you can be a stay-at-home mum *and* have a career
simultaneously, affording one or more foreign holidays a year? These
are wider vision-based goals. Whatever you wish to accomplish in
your life-time it is vital to dream. Human beings end up thriving
when they are striving towards something.

According to Australian nurse, Bronnie Ware, who spent several years
working in palliative care, caring for patients in the last 12 weeks of
their lives, the most common regret of all that she lists in her book,

The Top Five Regrets of the Dying, was "having had the courage to live a life true to myself, not the life others expected of me."

"When people realise that their life is almost over and look back clearly on it, it is easy to see how many dreams have gone unfulfilled," says Ware. "Most people had not honoured even a half of their dreams and had to die knowing that it was due to choices they had made, or not made. Health brings a freedom very few realise, until they no longer have it."

Indeed, being goal-oriented, true to yourself and having the courage to pursue your dreams are key determinants of success in life as they are in business. If you have clarity about what you want you can single-mindedly focus on achieving your goals each day rather than drifting around aimlessly. As founder of Piatkus Books, Judy Piatkus rightly points out, *"Being successful in business and life is about deciding on your goal and focusing on achieving it to the exclusion of all else."* In order to achieve your goals though, you need to first define them and then focus, work hard and persist. The direction you head in is solely determined by you, the goals you set, the thoughts that you think and the actions that you take towards realising your dreams. As such, to achieve your goals you must do three things:

1. **Clarify and set your goals.**
2. **Focus your mind.**
3. **Focus your actions.**

Your thoughts and dreams are, of course, only half of it. You need to DO as well as THINK. And, when obstacles, challenges, ginormous monsters of misfortune come along and slap you down; you must pick yourself up, dust yourself off and PERSIST. In doing so, you *will* achieve your goals. (We shall focus on the action and persistence part of achievement in the following Chapter).

"The best way to predict your future is to create it,"
Abraham Lincoln

"You are never too old to
set another goal or to dream a new dream,"
C.S. Lewis

OK, so, let's tackle these vital components of achievement step-by-step... LET'S DO THIS!

Clarify and Set Your Goals

1. **Clarify and set your goals.** Define your destination. Visualise where you wish to be and precisely what you wish to achieve.

    *   **Start by dreaming HUMUNGOUS!** If you could do/ achieve anything and were guaranteed to succeed (and money/time/experience was no object) what would you choose to be, to have or to do? This is a big question so take your time.

        Imagine you were granted a wish to create your dream life and write down your three biggest goals (add these to your My Dream Life worksheet on the next page).

    *   **Consider why you want what you want.** For example, say you list "a dream home of my own in such and such village." Ask yourself, what would having that give you? It might give you a safe hub and warm feeling that comes with security? It might give you a place to show off to your friends and impress people with when they come round for dinner? It might give you a feeling of having made it, which in turn would give you confidence, which in turn might give you peace-of-mind? Ask yourself what each thing gives you. It might give you a sense of belonging within a community and fulfil your purpose in life to help out in that community. There is always more to your desires than you think. Your dream home equals safety, security, confidence, belonging, meaning, happiness and so on.

- **Consider ways to create those feelings right now** (of safety, security, confidence, belonging, etc). For example, if the property you currently live in doesn't quite feel like home, do something about it so you can have a little of what you want right now. Devote Sunday to de-cluttering and blitzing the house or decorating or moving the furniture around to make it feel more like home. Get involved in your local community, volunteer, talk to your neighbours. Do something today and all week long that will give you the same feelings that you will have when you achieve your goal. It's a start. You can then start to formulate a plan to help you achieve your goal, but focus on this feeling first.

- **List your goals. Write your 'cosmic' shopping list.** Order your goals from the Shop of the Universe by writing your goals in the present tense, as if you have already achieved them. I know! This sounds weird but it helps to gain clarity and activates your subconscious mind into bringing opportunities, people and resources to you at the right time to enable you to achieve those goals.

  Let's say, for example, that you want to have earned enough money to buy your dream home by the end of the year. Instead of writing '2014 will be the year that I buy my own home' (in future tense) write: "I now own and live in my dream home" followed by the date by which you aim to achieve that goal.

  In 2003 I wrote down 'I have a book published, I am an author, I have met Anita Roddick,''... I ended up working towards achieving these goals and I secured a book deal, became an author and, not only met Dame Roddick but did some work for her promoting her website which led to her agreeing to write the Foreword to my book. Yippeee! Affirming goals in written form in the present tense is powerful. Go on. Write your cosmic shopping

My dream life

If money/time/experience was no object and
I could do ANYTHING, I would:

1. _____

2. _____

3. _____

My cosmic shopping list for 2014

Goal (Date)

e.g. We have saved a deposit so can now afford to buy our dream home (Dec 2014)

_____

_____

_____

_____

_____

_____

list of goals right here. You've got nothing to lose and oh so very much to gain. (Commit them to your very own 'My Dream Life' worksheet).

- **Double check that pursuing your goals will be worth it.** Before you invest immense energy and time into achieving your goals make sure you ask yourself: is this something you really want? Do you enjoy doing this and are you likely to continue to enjoy it? Will any sacrifices you may have to make in order to achieve your goal be worth it? (For example if you are aiming to achieve a certain level within your career, is the pressure you may be under and the occasional lack of family time worth the end result?) Make sure you're fully aware of what you're letting yourself in for then, if you are certain that you want this more than anything – go for it.

- **Share your goals with everybody.** That way you will become accountable for them, and you'll notice that opportunities will arise that help you bring them to fruition.

"If you want to live a happy life, tie it to a goal, not to people or things."
Albert Einstein

Focus on Your Vision

2. **Focus your mind.** Believe that you can and you will. Let go of self-doubt, it doesn't serve you. If you believe you can't achieve something then you won't. Simple. Your self-doubt will become a self-fulfilling prophecy and your dreams will be shattered. Conversely, if you have faith in yourself and your abilities to achieve your goals, you WILL do it. You know you deserve to. But it is up to you, nobody else. You – and only YOU - are entirely responsible. It's all up to you and your belief and faith that these goals can and will be achieved.

The secret is to keep transmitting this belief out to the Universe. If you are like any normal human-being anywhere, doubt will occasionally creep in to your mind, yet, as it does so, the danger is that you break that transmission. As soon as you put it out there that you don't have what you want, that's what you get – NOT having what you want. But if you transmit that you do have what you want … that's what you'll get. That is the key, making your dreams a reality in your mind's eye and maintaining that feeling of gratitude for having your hearts desire, without ever breaking that transmission, without doubting.

- **Create your future in your mind's eye as if is already your present.** Visualise having already achieved your goals, as if they were already a reality. This is an extension of writing down your goals as if you've achieved them but goes one step further. Picture yourself having achieved them. Feel – and I mean *really feel* - how you would feel if it were so; experience the excitement and emotion and joy that fulfilling your dreams has brought you; vividly and clearly see yourself enjoying your accomplishment. If your goal is to write a book, picture yourself walking into your local book shop and seeing your book on the shelf. Pick it up and feel the cover; feel the emotions you'd feel. If your goal is to buy your dream home; create a mental picture and emotion combination; see yourself living there, enjoying coffee in the kitchen or watching your children play in the garden. Feel the emotion that accompanies the image. This combination has tremendous impact and activates the universal "Law of Attraction" which delivers to you all you need to achieve your goal, because you are more likely to attract into your life the things you think about and focus on.

Ask for it and you create it. Then believe that it's right here. Imagine that you can feel it, smell it, touch it, live it. It's yours. Know that. Focus hard on that feeling of actually having what you want right now. Visualise it. See it right here in your mind's eye. Concentrate on that vision and on that feeling; make it real. Do this often. The Universe shall deliver. Do this first before spending any time figuring out *how* to make that vision into a reality. Make it a reality in your mind. Believe that it has already happened first.

Using your imagination and rewiring your mind to have complete and utter faith and constantly believing and feeling and knowing that you have what you want and even pretending that you already have it, that it's here (it's on its way) – that's powerful. Make believe that it's true, feel its truth and, as you do that more than questioning whether it will ever happen, as you shift away from that questioning into the realms of belief, it WILL HAPPEN. Shift the balance from doubting and questioning towards knowing and believing. It takes practice but it's worth it when you master that unwavering belief and complete faith.

For example, do you want more money? Imagine buying the things you would love to have if you had more money for your loved ones. Picture it. Believe that it has happened and that you are living that life. Do this often enough that your imagined reality penetrates your subconscious mind because, when that happens, you will receive and achieve it.

As Rhonda Byrne explains in *The Secret Daily Teachings*, the more you know and understand that you will get what you have asked for and the less you question and worry about receiving it, the more likely it will happen.

"Imagine writing an email of what you want to the Universe. When you are happy that your email is very clear, you hit 'Send' and you know your request has gone into the ethers. You also know that the Server of the

Universe is an automatic system, and it doesn't question email requests. Its job is simply to fulfil every request.

If you begin to worry and stress that you haven't got what you wanted, then you have just sent another email to the Universe to STOP YOUR ORDER. And then you wonder why you haven't received what you asked for.

Once you Ask, know that the Server of the Universe is an automatic infallible system that never fails, and expect to receive your request!"

- **Affirm your goals by saying them out loud.** I often do this while walking the dog or driving the car (when nobody is around so I don't look like a complete loon). And don't fret if you don't achieve your goal in the time scale that you've specified; just set a new deadline. As Brian Tracy says, "There are no unreasonable goals, only unreasonable deadlines." Another way to do this is to tell the story of you achieving your goal. For example, "I'm just so thrilled to see my children's book published. I walked into Waterstones and there it was on the shelf next to The Hungry Caterpillar. I could hardly believe it, but then I did persist, even when I felt like giving up after receiving so many rejection letters. Thankfully, a publisher fell in love with the story. It took them a couple of months to respond, but they did, and now I'm a published children's author."

I am

I have

I am willing to

I am in the process of

"Money doesn't bring happiness – but happiness brings money,"
Rhonda Byrne

My Affirmations

All is well in our world

The three of us are healthy and well

My latest book is a global best-seller

We have moved into our new home

We regularly enjoy eating al fresco
in our garden

All is well in our world.

My Affirmations

- **Write down your perfect day where the achievement of all of your dreams come together into a wonderful ideal 24 hours.** Imagine what it would actually be like to be living your dream. When do you wake up and what do you see? What do you do next? What's for breakfast? Then what? How do you spend your morning, lunchtime, afternoon and evening? Describe what you are doing, who you are with and how this makes you feel. Get specific. Make it real. Write non-stop for a few minutes about what you see, feel, hear and smell. Do it here:

MY PERFECT DAY

Now imagine it as real. Have a lie down. Relax, breathe deeply and imagine your future. Picture your future desk, examine your environment, what colours catch your eye? What sounds? Breathe in your surroundings. Now focus on what you're doing. Who is there with you? Why are you smiling? What are you enjoying? What are you achieving? Imagine yourself telling someone else about how proud you feel about achieving something. See your success. Feel it. Look at your future bank statement. See the

My story of success

I did it! Here's my description:

(e.g. I'm sat in my red-carpeted lounge, looking at the bookshelf in front of me, sipping my freshly made coffee. I notice three books on the lowest shelf, all written by me. My awards are on the top shelf & a royalty cheque sits on the coffee table. So let me tell you how it happened...)

_____

_____

_____

_____

_____

_____

_____

_____

_____

_____

_____

pile of cheques on your desk, the awards on your shelves, the certificates on your wall, the photo of your smiling child on the side. Now sit up, get out your notepad and pen and fill in any gaps in your PERFECT DAY notes above. Revisit and read this often, close your eyes and visualise it.

Here's an example of the Story of Success that I wrote before submitting this very book:

> I'm so happy to have achieved my goal of writing a best-seller and to be following my purpose to empower others to achieve their goals, reach their potential and boost their well-being. I'm standing out from the crowd by providing *practical* action-focused guidance. From my workspace I can see my garden filled with lavender bushes, books I've written & awards I've won.

As well as completing the detailed story above try summarising in a few sentences as I did:

I am so happy to have achieved my goal of _____

and be following my passion to _____.

I am standing out from the crowd by being _____.

From my workspace I can see _____.

- **Create a vision board to capture what your vision looks like.** (e.g. your children and you in your dream kitchen or garden; speaking at an event where you reveal how you 'made it'; relaxing on a holiday that your business enabled you to afford). Get a bunch of magazines and cut out images that appeal to your vision. Gather photos or graphics of sunshine, beaches, homewares symbolising your dream home. Here's mine:

Include images that symbolise or capture your dreams, goals, purpose and also stuff that makes you smile. Pin it in a place where you will look at it frequently.

*"All you have to do is know where you are going.
The answers will come to you of their own accord,"*
Earl Nightingale

- Create a Creative Business Collage/Vision Board if you run your own business.

  - Grab a pile of magazines and/or surf the web/use Pinterest.com. Cut or print out words and images that inspire you; that symbolise or summarise what you and your customers do, your business purpose, who your customers are, what you strive for, how you see your business and brand, where you wish to be, where you hope your business will take you, what benefits you aim to provide your customers with, and so on.

- Write on a brightly coloured post-it notes your 'elevator pitch'. This is a summary of your value proposition, something that you could say to pitch your idea to a potential investor or partner in a lift or 'elevator' before they reach their floor and leave you and your opportunity behind. It's essentially what your business is/does in a nutshell; incorporating your mission, vision and values.

My business is a _____ for _____

who have a problem with _____.

Its core goal is to _____by

providing _____ that stand out/

are uniquely differentiated from the competition by

being _____.

- Jot down some inspirational quotes for guidance and interesting statistics that give weight to your business proposition and justify why you do what you do.

- Write on another post-it note I AM _____ (followed by three or four affirmations. e.g. "I AM: healthy, happy, helpful and successful".)

- Cut out a few photographs or images of two or three things you hope to achieve as a result of having a successful business, whether this is your dream home, a Caribbean holiday or something else.

- Stick all of this onto a large piece of card to craft your very own Creative Business Collage.

- Place it above your computer screen/desk.

Here's my Creative Business Vision Board Collage for my business, WiBBLE (Women in Business: Brilliant Local Enterprises) www.WiBBLE.us

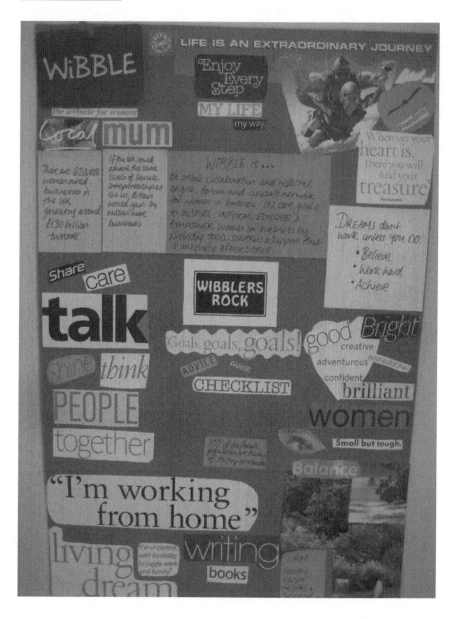

- Understand why failure is your friend. As leading self-help author and motivational speaker, Brian Tracy says, "Successful people fail far more often than unsuccessful people. Successful people try more things, fall down, pick themselves up and try again — over and over before they finally win." Remember, your defeats define you and fuel you. We all make mistakes. As Winston Churchill famously said, "Success is going from failure to failure without losing enthusiasm." It's how we react to the things we botch which can determine how successful we will be. Successful people view failure as feedback and mistakes are merely learning tools, providing insight to enable more informed choices as we progress through life. Learning lessons the hard way can be a better (albeit more painful) way of learning. Because those lessons stick. See failure as USEFUL and you will never be afraid of trying or failing (which, by the way is better than not trying and doing nothing).

- Understand the 'why?' Set your core goals to achieve this month, quarter, year. But ask yourself 'why'? Goal-achievement becomes easier when you've sussed out your motivation. What's your emotional trigger?

- For example, says GB Women's team basketball coach, Nick Grantham, about the GB team: "What is the reason they're doing this? It's never just to win, it's to fulfil a dream, like making their family proud or overcoming adversity."

- What's your inspiration? What's your 'why?' Write it on your inspiration sheet here:

My inspiration is

(e.g. to make my family proud; to set a good example for my daughter; to leave a legacy behind; to positively impact the lives of others and make a real difference in the world; to empower and inspire as many people as is humanly possible; to have written a book that I myself would like to read).

_____

_____

_____

_____

_____

_____

_____

_____

_____

_____

_____

_____

TO DO LIST AND PLANNER

Write Cosmic *
SHOPPING LIST
_____

Cut out magazine
pics + Print photos

Write My
Story of Success

Create Vision
Boards for LIFE
+ BIZ

FLOURISH PLANNER (ongoing)

Schedule in:
- Affirmations on a daily/weekly basis.
- Visualisation of goals having been achieved on a daily/ weekly basis.

Printable Quotes... to cut out n stick up

"Vision without action is merely a dream. Action without vision just passes the time. Vision WITH action can change the world!"

Joel A. Barker

"It is a terrible thing to see and have no vision."

Helen Keller

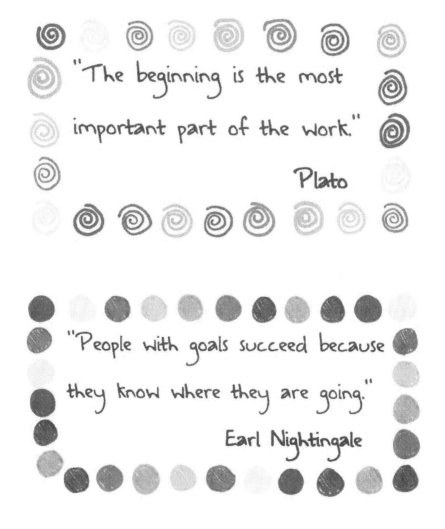

"The beginning is the most important part of the work."

Plato

"People with goals succeed because they know where they are going."

Earl Nightingale

Chapter 10

MONTH Ten: Self-Discipline and Persistence

Focusing On Action To Get Results

So far you've sketched out your vision and affirmed your wildest dreams; you've defined and clarified your goals so you know exactly where you are headed. You've explored what you want and why you want it. Crucially, you now need to figure out how to get there. You need a map to take you towards your destination, a plan of action to guide you in the right direction. It's far easier to stay passionate about where you are headed if you know how you are going to get there.

So, while your dreams should be WILD, your plans should be REAL. Plans are the stepping stones towards your wildest dreams, a sequence of logical actions that take you step-by-step from where you are now to where you wish to be. And, even if your dreams seem illogical or impossible, no matter. Because, in taking those active steps towards them, you are heading in the right direction; you are growing, and that, my friend, is an enjoyable path to be on. Enjoy that journey. Keep dreaming wild dreams. But vitally, make and act on your plans.

But hey! I have some good news for you! You don't necessarily need to make ginormous changes or take gigantic steps. You can start by taking small simple steps towards your dreams. In doing so you are already closer to your goal than you were and the change has already begun. If one of your goals is to lose weight, if you just change one small thing (take the stairs instead of the lift, or swap one daily snack for fruit or veg, or drink an extra glass of water each day or reduce your tea-time portion size) that's one step towards achieving your goal. It's manageable rather than unattainable action making it more likely and able to happen. And, more good news. If you continue to do that one thing differently, to make that small change, for 21 days, you'll create a brand new good habit to replace your old pattern of behaviour. 21 days is how long it takes your neural pathways to shift. That's not very long. So do something different, no matter how small. Just do SOMETHING.

It's easy to dream. Being disciplined and persistent enough to take action is less easy. One of the main regrets of the dying is that they wish they'd pursued their dreams instead of coming to the end of their lives and thinking regretfully, 'I wish I'd done that'. Dreams don't work unless you do, so figure out a way to take action towards that goal and persist each day to make it happen.

Dreams remain in your head until you plan and take action. Apparently, to become world class at something you would need to spend 60 hours per week on practising that skill over a ten year period. I'm not suggesting that you aim to become a world class Olympian or the best in the world at any particular skill by devoting a decade of long weeks to become the best of the best. However, you will need to exercise effort, self-control and skill in order to turn the seeds of your dreams into flourishing flowers of reality.

So, let's explore how to create an achievable action plan and stick to it.

1. **Focus your actions**. Your vision is only half of it. You need to DO as well as THINK.

   - **Create an action plan and take daily action steps**. Your plan should outline EXACTLY what you need to do in order to achieve your goals, step-by-step, action-by-action. So be specific. List knowledge to learn, skills to develop, obstacles to overcome and so on.

- o Refer back to your 'My Dream Life' and 'Cosmic Shopping List' Worksheet/Page. These are your goals that you need to take action towards.
- o Include small steps/actions, whether that's doing 15 minutes worth of exercise, drinking water half an hour before your lunch, telling someone why you appreciate them or practising a skill that you have, include those action steps in your plan.
- o Plot the tasks that need to happen to achieve those goals in My Action Plan on pages 224-225. There's one for each area of your life (WORK – Biz/Career and LIFE – Environment/Family+Friends/Health/ Energy/Fun).
- o Give each task an achievable deadline. Listing the required steps will reveal that your goal is more attainable than you may have envisaged. Planning is vital. Writing down your goal, creating a plan and then taking focused action increases your chances of achieving your goals tenfold.

  The bottom line? If you engage in consistent action and take a step towards your goal every single day – you WILL reach your destination.

"A journey of a thousand miles begins with a single step,"
Lao Tzu

- **Prioritise these tasks based on their logical sequence** (which need to be done first/in which order) **and importance** (rather than their urgency). Consider which task you would do if you were only allowed to choose one. Focusing on your most important tasks until they are complete with no distraction will boost your productivity.

- **Focus on the most effective tasks.** Assess which 80% of goal-achieving results come from which 20% of your activities. Schedule in more of those actions. Goal power!

- **Learn.** Devote time to learning whatever you need to in order to reach your goals. Remember this, ALL experts were once novices! What do you need to learn, improve, do or overcome. Write it down here.

I need to improve my _____ skills

My biggest challenge/obstacle is: _____

My purpose is: _____
Eg: to help 20,000 people to boost their well-being and flourish by the end of 2015.

My vision is: _____
My new home and continuing to live my dream of working from that home.

My motivation is: _____
To create an amazing garden for my family by the end of 2014.

- **Reward yourself.** We give our children stars and rewards for good behaviour, so why not reward yourself for completing a task, particularly one that you are not motivated to complete? By writing down or drawing a picture of your chosen reward that you will give yourself when the job is done, you are more likely to get on and do it.

MY REWARD

WHEN I ACHIEVE (insert goal)

I WILL REWARD MYSELF WITH

My Action Plan

WORK/CAREER/BIZ GOALS

- Help 5,000+ people to achieve their goals
- Get a book published

ACTIONABLE TASKS	Deadline
Research/data dump/organise chapters	Jan 31
Write book proposal and sample material	Feb 4
Submit to publishers	Feb 4
Finish writing draft manuscript	Mar 1
Investigate self-publishing options	Mar 15
Set up mailing list on website	Mar 30

My Action Plan

LIFE GOALS

- Spend more time with people who make me feel good

- Be more patient

- Find more energy

ACTIONABLE TASKS   Deadline

Get more sleep

Eat better foods do weekly meal – planner including snacks

Contract positive peeps to schedule in time to see each other

- **Review whether your actions over the past few hours have tied in with your wider goals, projects and purpose.** When you see that the majority of what you are doing, even seemingly unrelated activities, are consistent with your life's purpose and are giving your life significance, you'll feel a warm sense of well-being. If you find your actions are less consistent with your goals, you can simply bring yourself back on track by regaining focus and find harmony as a result.

- **Break down those main tasks into individual tasks.** For example 'complete book manuscript' would be broken down into 'write chapter 10', 'write chapter 11', 'proofread and edit', etc...or App Development would be broken down into 'draw storyboard for app customer journey', 'phone app developers to book meetings', etc. You could then give those individual daily tasks dates.

- **Create a Post-it Note Plan Schedule**
    - Group the tasks in your action plan into the month in which they need to be actioned.
    - Then group them into three or four key areas, such as 1) marketing/promotion, 2) website content and development 3) launch event or 1) publishing options 2) learning/research/e-course 3) app/web development 4) marketing/content.
    - Create a calendar for the month ahead (see below) with mini sticky note size spaces for each day. Write each of your three or four grouped task headings onto colour coded large sticky notes – a different colour sticky note for each grouped task to put down the right hand side of your planner.
    - Break down these group tasks (as above) into individual daily tasks and colour code them around these three/four group task areas. You will no doubt have a good deal more than one or two tasks to carry out each day;

but this action-oriented sticky note planner will enable you to focus on the most vital tasks which will each get you closer to achieving your main goals, as set out.

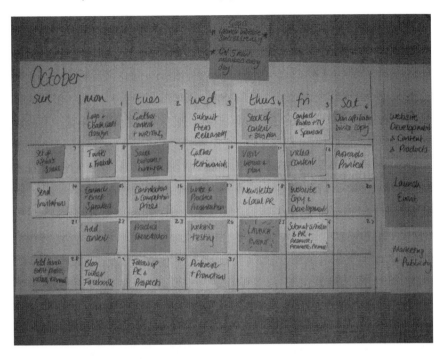

The core goals were to launch a website and get five new members every day. The three key areas were: Website Development/Content and Products, Launch Event, Marketing and Publicity.

Today = A Good Day

My Goals

1.
2.
3.

My Affirmations

1.
2.
3.

7am
8am
9am
10am
11am
12pm
1pm
2pm
3pm
4pm
5pm
6pm
7pm
8pm
9pm
10pm
11pm

Note: The Ultimate Flourish Planner at the end of the book will help you.

2. **Persist.** When obstacles, challenges and great ginormous giant monsters of misfortune come along and slap you down; you pick yourself up, dust yourself off and you PERSIST. In doing so, you will achieve your goals.

- **Resolve to never give up on the right dream.** Write it here. Do it now.

I promise to never give up on my dream. I deserve to achieve it and I will do so. Your turn:

"Perseverance is not a long race; it is many short races one after another,"
Walter Elliott (Priest and Missionary)

- **Pivot and change direction though, if needs be.** Have the courage of your convictions. That includes having the courage to change course when you feel you are going down the wrong track. Shifting direction by being true to yourself isn't failure or giving up, it's just changing course and taking a different route when you come up against a road block or dead end. While persistence, determination and effort are required when pursuing dreams, it would be crazy to persist at pursuing the wrong dream or trying to do something you're just not cut out for and, in doing so, banging your head against a brick wall, just because you don't want to give up. It's not giving up if you pursue the right dream with equal vigour. It's only giving up if you can't be bothered to do hard work even at something that you're good at, or is right for you. Follow your heart but don't be afraid to adapt, shift direction and do something different in order to pursue what is right for you. Some of the most successful people have pivoted, from Moshi Monster creator Michael Action-Smith to Moo.com founder, Richard Moross and Sir Richard Branson.

- **Take calculated risks to make informed decisions.** Don't jump blindly. Follow your instincts, do some research and, by all-means be a risk-taker, just make sure you have some awareness about the potential pros and cons of what you are about to do. The very nature of risk taking means that you are doing something that you cannot be certain will work out, but it is worthwhile stacking the odds in your favour by trusting your intuition and knowing the consequences of a decision before launching forth.

- **Be resilient**. If at first you don't succeed, try and try again. Successful people have often failed more than once but have bounced back. Failure and mistakes merely equipped them with the tools to do things better next time and spurred them onwards. Resilience and tenacity are important traits for flourishers to possess. Obstacles and objections are there to be overcome. Be prepared to go the extra mile. JK Rowling's first submission of Harry Potter was rejected, not just once but twice by now-kicking-themselves publishers. She didn't give up. The third submission was accepted and JK Rowling is now the most successful children's author ever. It is very rare to hear a story of great achievement without a story leading up to that achievement of rejection and hindrance. Some say FAIL is an acronym for First Attempt In Learning. I love that!

> *"Take chances, make mistakes. That's how*
> *you grow. Pain nourishes your courage.*
> *You have to fail in order to practice being brave."*
> **Mary Tyler Moore**

> *"Success is made up of 99% failure. You galvanize yourself,*
> *and you keep going, as a full optimist,"* **James Dyson**

Enjoy The Journey of Growth

While the destination is a crucial part of the plan (it's why you are taking action, it's the end game, the dream that is propelling you forward) the destination is not the b-all and end-all. The JOURNEY towards that destination is equally as important, if not more so. You must take time to ENJOY THE JOURNEY! Reaching your destination will give you a sense of achievement and a temporary feeling of enormous well-being. However the actual process of working towards that goal SHOULD give you as much well-being as reaching that goal. If it doesn't you are setting yourself up for a fall. Here's why:

1. **Enjoy the journey of growth.** The problem with us human-beings is that we tend to focus on our future happiness rather

than our current contentment. As outlined in Chapter Eight, we often think, "I'll be happy when..." So "I'll be happy when I'm in our dream home,"... "I'll be happy when I weigh 9 stone/get that new car/find that new job" ... "I'll be happy when I achieve this goal or that goal." It's a constant striving for something that we believe will make us happier than we are now. Unfortunately, what tends to happen is that the novelty wears off so, while achieving a goal fills us with blissful feelings of accomplishment and glory... that soon wears off, not entirely, but slightly. It's a temporary state of happiness that is soon replaced by the need to achieve something else, the need to strive for some new goal. What actually generates long-lasting happiness is the PROCESS of working towards that goal, the actual GROWTH, the thrill of the chase if you like. We love to get better at things, to learn, to train, to collect, to earn money to save towards something. It's the process of striving, the growth towards that goal-attainment that boosts well-being. That is why setting and working towards goals is important when it comes to well-being. It's not just *reaching* our potential and achieving our goals that brings us joy, but taking each step to get us there. As Gretchen Rubin says in *The Happiness Project*, "This hedonic treadmill, as it's called, makes it easy to grow accustomed to some of the things that make you 'feel good', such as a new car, a new job title, or air-conditioning, so that the good feeling wears off. An atmosphere of growth offsets that. You may soon take your new dining table for granted, but tending your garden will give you fresh joy and surprise every spring."

Dreams and goals are your garden of happiness. Their seeds are planted in your mind and, with each step you take towards achieving them, you water those seeds and they FLOURISH gradually over time so that, when you reach your goal/make your dream come true it represents a flower in full-bloom. This provides you as much happiness as the process of watering and tending to that flower as it goes from seedling to first bud to blossoming flower. But the flower doesn't last forever in bloom, it fades, and you need to start again, tending to those dreams – your very own seedlings of reality.

That is why:

- At the end of this chapter on page 134 you shall find a fabulous 'my journey worksheet' to help you to enjoy the journey and the very process of flourishing; of walking step-by-step towards your dreams.
- You should always include learning, creating/building/ developing something and even teaching into your action plans. Schedule in time to grow and enjoy the process of growth.

> *"Happiness is neither virtue nor pleasure nor this thing nor that, but simply GROWTH. We are happy when we are growing,"*
> **William Butler Yeats**

While the arrival fallacy and 'hedonic treadmill' concept reveals that achievement and goals can be over-focused on, this does not mean that goal-achievement is over-rated. On the contrary – having, pursuing and achieving goals is fruitful; a key component of flourishing. Achieving a goal is just as valid as the process of achieving it. The secret is to enjoy the journey towards your goals and revel in the anticipation of achievement. Dream big but don't let ambition dampen your current state-of-contentment.' Pursue and accept. Dream but feel content now too, especially given that you are working towards your dreams.

So many people forget to enjoy that growth journey by focusing too hard on the end result. Soak up the joy of the journey – each step, each moment, because that moment (and that one) is your life. Cherish watering your seeds, watch them flourish and you will too.

It's important to have a firm idea of what we'd like to accomplish during our lifetime. Having a clear vision of what we wish to attain spurs us on, gives our lives meaning and purpose and becomes a yardstick for measuring how well we are doing. This striving to achieve stuff only becomes problematic if you stop enjoying the journey towards it. If your fixation on the future reduces your pleasure within the present, it's not worth it. If you do that your chance of living a happy life is reduced. It's absolutely critical to enjoy the journey, to reward yourself along the way for mini-milestones, to enjoy experiences TODAY, to feel gratified RIGHT NOW (hence the importance of optimising experience, as explored in Chapter 5). Get rid of the belief that all meaning and gratification will take place in the future, because that simply postpones happiness. As is often said, 'you might get run over by a bus tomorrow.' You probably won't, but now is where it's at – happiness, well-being, contentment. Pat yourself on the back for growing and for, just, being.

The problem is that people get confused. They see goals and a wider purpose as something to work towards; a vision as something that they are striving for, as something that will happen in the future. And while this is true, this actually means that simply by having a clear purpose and vision today, you are giving meaning to your life NOW, you are ensuring that your actions, activities and experiences that you are living right at this moment have significance. That fact should enable you to enjoy your journey towards your destination, because everything you are doing has meaning and significance and is worth celebrating immediately. So stop postponing your happiness in lieu of achieving your goals and enjoy the moment, the steps you are taking, the journey. Enjoy the very process of living, the stream of experiences that spur you on. Harvest the rewards for living today.

I'm moving in the right direction, step-by-step... I'm growing! :-)

My Journey

Ready, Steady, GROW!

Stuff I've done this week on my journey towards my goals:

_____

_____

_____

_____

_____

_____

_____

I've enjoyed this process because:

_____

_____

_____

_____

_____

TO DO LIST AND PLANNER

 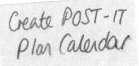

FLOURISH PLANNER (ongoing)

Schedule in:
- Daily or weekly completion of MY JOURNEY worksheet.
- Monthly creation of Post-It Plan Schedule.

Printable Quotes... to cut out n stick up

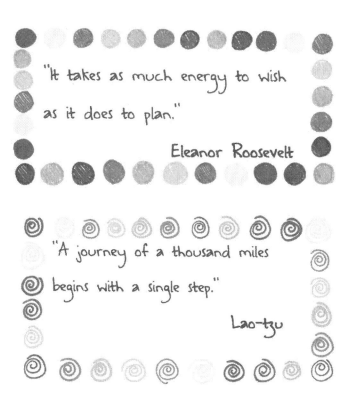

Perseverance is not a long race; it is many short races one after another."

Walter Elliott

I can't change the direction of the wind, but I can adjust my sails to always reach my destination."

Jimmy Dean

Chapter 11

MONTH ELEVEN:
Master Time Management

Create More Time and Get More Done

*"Time is the coin of your life. It is the only coin you have,
and only you can determine how it will be spent. Be
careful lest you let other people spend it for you,"*
Carl Sandbur

Lack of time is constantly cited as a major barrier to success. Yup, not having enough hours in the day is a persistent problem. It can be tough to make the most of our time, to optimise it and enable ourselves to take time out to relax and unwind. Cramming everything in can leave us inpatient and grouchy and feeling like we've got nowhere. Furthermore, if you run your own business or provide a service in your job, time is money. Yet, everything generally ends up taking longer than you think it will. The secret to mastering time management is good planning. Breaking your time into chunks and gaining clarity on what needs to be done then creating a manageable and achievable routine is the way forward.

So here are some ways to help you create at least one more hour per day by using your time wisely.

1. **Use Pareto's Principle to prioritise your to-do list.** Focus on the tasks that have the most impact, both in terms of generating the best results within your work and generating the most well-being within your life. To do this you can use the Pareto Principle aka the 80/20 rule which Pareto established when 80% of Italian land was owned by 20%

of the population. The Pareto principle suggests that it is 20% of our efforts which brings in 80% of our rewards, so, in business, 20% of our customers/efforts brings in 80% of our income and, in life, 20% of our activities/efforts bring in 80% of our happiness.

- **Trim down your to-do list to include between three to five top priority tasks to complete each day.** See page 228. Look back at your diaries. Which 20% of your efforts are accomplishing something or making you feel good? Which tasks are generating the best results and highest level of well-being? Get analytical. If you run your own business or are in a career where certain tasks generate specific results, examine which 20% of your customers/ efforts are bringing in the most revenue/results by looking back over your annual sales figures and/or your targets/results. It could be specific customers or specific customer groups (e.g. hairdressers or parents of children under 4 or people based in a certain location). You then know who to focus your promotional activities on and who to contact to see if they are ready to buy from you again or refer business your way.

  Furthermore, you can look at which of your activities are generating the most reward or highest ROI (return on investment), whether that's networking, gaining PR coverage, making follow-up calls or updating your website. Prioritise your tasks based on which will result in the most positive impact for you and your business (if you are self-employed). Eliminate tasks which bring little monetary benefit to the business or little reward to your weekly results/targets/achievements.

- **Prioritise non-work related tasks in the same way.** Which tasks are most important in terms of giving you and your family a sense of well-being? For instance playing with your children and taking them swimming or picking up from school and reading to them, may be preferable to cleaning the house or taking the bins out. As such you could delegate those low-score tasks or plan to do them together to enable more 'play' time. Or, because you are optimising your business/work results by prioritising effectively, you could use the extra cash to hire a cleaner for an hour or two each week or fortnight. You may not be able to eliminate all tasks that don't boost your well-being (such as ironing), but you can get an even balance by doing more activities that do. (Or hire someone to iron those shirts from time to time).

2. **Break down your day into 45 minute, hourly or 90 minute blocks so that you can create a strict routine.** In between these blocks include blocks of other tasks, such as exercising, paperwork, lunch, phone calls, meeting friends, going for a walk, reading, doing flourishing activities that appear on your 'what I love to do' list or the 100 pick n mix flourishing activity sheet. See Chapter 12 for your Ultimate Flourishing Planner which enables you to schedule everything into those clear blocks of time.

   - **Focus by giving yourself blasts of allocated time for certain tasks.** Focus on your prioritised tasks for at least 45-60 minutes at a time and get rid of other distractions while you genuinely focus on completing each of the three to five top priority tasks on your list. Switch off your Skype and instant messaging, step away from Facebook and close your e-mail or any other distractions during that set time. If you really must, once that 45-60 minutes is up, go and check your social media/e-mail. Then get back into the zone and focus for another chunk of time. This really works.

   - **Schedule in certain tasks each day to avoid them interfering with your prioritised ones.** So, for example, plan your social media activity to take place at times when they are most effective. According to Bit.ly the best times to post on social media sites are generally first thing in the morning and then between 6-8pm GMT, depending on your time-zone. Find out your most responsive time to post based on the engagement your posts generate and, if it's between 8-10am and 6-8pm, avoid going on Facebook in between those times. The same applies with e-mails. Schedule in time to check and respond to your e-mails in the morning, at lunch time and again at the end of the day, not continuously hitting the send/receive button as most people generally do.

- **Divide tasks into type.** For example, if you run your own business, 'marketing' might include content creation, social media management, press release distribution, forum posts 'Sales and distribution' might include making prospect and follow-up calls, presentation creation, Skype meetings, packaging and posting products to customers. You'll also need to factor in time to actually create what you are selling, whether that's making or sourcing a product or carrying out a service. Now divide these types into regular daily time slots. Schedule in some me time and some learning time and some goal-achieving actions to take you closer to your goals. For example:

9am   MARKETING: Social media marketing and check emails

10am   MARKETING: Content creation

11am   SALES/DISTRIBUTION: Product/service action

12.30   Lunch

1pm   SALES/DISTRIBUTION: Sales calls/Skype meetings/ email replies

2pm   SALES/DISTRIBUTION: Product/service action / Distribution

3pm   STOP. Down tools, collect kids, be mum

8pm   MARKETING: Social media marketing/email replies

9pm   Me-time and/or learning time and/or goal-achieving action

Obviously this won't work every day. Sometimes you have to be reactive rather than pro-active and react to an urgent enquiry or emergency or catch up on cleaning or admin or other less productive tasks. Scheduling does enable focus though – and focus is a clear time-optimiser.

3. **Create more time and become a time detective.** There is only so much time in the day. But there are ways you can maximise your time by being more productive, spending your time more wisely and cutting out time that is wasted. Time to catch those time-thieves.

- **Examine your diary.** Seek out wasted pockets of time. Minutes here and there which could be more effectively spent. List those chunks of time and what you do with them and jot down how you could better spend that time. For example, you may find yourself checking your email every ten minutes, going on Facebook constantly, browsing online shopping sites, reading blogs that don't really serve you, devoting large chunks of time to tidying up instead of clearing as you go, and so on.

- **Harness the power of technology to track where you might be losing time.** For example www.RescueTime.com informs you which websites or programmes you spend the most time on, so that you can discover which areas you need to address. There is also a tool which restricts the time you spend on Facebook: www.facebooklimiter.com. Try www.Evernote.com to jot down whatever is on your mind and create online notebooks for different topics. You can even clip articles you find together to read later, when you have some spare time available (e.g. when you might have previously just watched TV).

- **Reduce unproductive time.** Cut back on face to face meetings that may be unnecessary. Have meetings online where possible using gotomeeting.com or Skype rather than spending time getting to a meeting, parking the car, having the meeting and returning to your workplace.

- **Delegate and outsource.** People often limit themselves and place restrictions on what they are able to achieve in a single day by thinking they can't afford to outsource or hire someone else to do work for them. I have two things to say about that:

  1) **It need not cost the earth.** There are a whole bunch of fabulous sites brimming with people who are keen to do stuff for you for a tiny cost. Why? Because they want to build up their portfolio of work (eg logo designers, illustrators, web developers, and so on) and/or they hope that, if they impress you with their quality of work now, you may use them as you become more able to afford them (eg virtual assistance, book-keepers, cleaning service providers and so on). Check out: www.fiverr.com or www.fivesquids.co.uk (for specific one off jobs which cost just $5 or £5). www.Odesk.com (top quality but low cost developers). Also look at www.freelancers.co.uk, www.peopleperhour.com, www.elance.com, www.getafreelancer.com.
  2) Decide whether to outsource based on your aspirations (where you want to be) rather than pragmatical reasons (where you are now).

- **Get organised.** Reduce the amount of time you spend looking for files, searching for paperwork, hunting for your keys/wallet/bag. Dedicate an hour this week to organising your computer files into relevant folders, deleting emails and saving important ones in relevant folders, filing paperwork in specific folders and creating a dedicated space for your keys and wallet where you always put them without fail. Know where things are.

Once you have a clear desk/inbox/computer, you can plan more effectively. Planning is vital to flourishing. Remember "luck is where preparation meets opportunity". If you run your own business, you can benefit from the WiBBLE Business Toolkit (disclaimer: WiBBLE is my own business). There are a range of nifty planners and worksheets to help you, including a wall planner, marketing planner, PR planner. Plus there's an Achieve Your Goals worksheet to help you stay on track. Visit http://www.WiBBLE.us/register.

If you can save an hour a day, that's an increase in productivity of over 31 full days per year! – That's one whole month 'created' – a month that you can use to plan, think, relax, take a holiday, read, learn, and FLOURISH. :-) Yippeee!

To Do List and Planner

Examine previous DIARIES - Find 20% most effective tasks & time-thieves

Examine social media insights to assess BEST TIME to post stuff

Check out ODESK.com FIVERR.com, PEOPLEPERHOUR.com etc..

FLOURISH PLANNER (ongoing)

Schedule in:
- Creating a daily prioritised to-do list of three to five daily tasks based on Pareto's principles. See printables below.
- Weekly planning – filling out the Ultimate Flourish Planner (see next chapter) based on 45-90 minute blocks of time.

Printable Quotes... to cut out n stick up

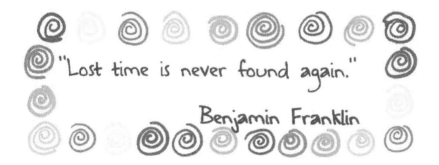

"Lost time is never found again."

Benjamin Franklin

"Time = Life. Therefore,

waste your time and

waste of your life,

or master your time and

master your life."

Alan Lakein

Chapter 12

MONTH TWELVE:
Plan To Flourish

Your ULTIMATE FLOURISH PLANNER

This is where your WELLBEING WORK takes proper shape and you can put all that you have learned from the pages of this handbook into action.

Having defined your destination and written down your goals and actions you'll need to take in order to achieve those goals, it's time to schedule all of these actions, along with a whole bunch of flourishing activities into your weekly schedule, into your ULTIMATE FLOURISH PLANNER.

By using this planner you will not only schedule in tasks that will enable you to achieve your goals and reach your potential, you will also boost your well-being by scheduling in activities that will make you feel more positive emotion, more engagement, help you pursue your purpose, give your life meaning and make you feel happier (for example by seeing more of the 'feel good' friends you enjoy spending time with and doing more of the activities that you absolutely love to do). You'll schedule in time to be grateful, exercise, recharge your batteries and empower yourself to head in the right direction and enjoy the journey.

This weekly schedule – your ULTIMATE FLOURISH PLANNER should include:
- Action-steps towards your goals
- Happiness-inducing activities that you and your loved ones love to do (family-time, team-time, me-time, switch-off time, mindful time, etc.)

- Social bonding moments with your friends and family
- Energising time.
- Work time.
- Chores time.
- Planning time (so that you schedule in all of this).

Furthermore, you'll need to include the ongoing actions and tasks from each chapter/month. I've listed them here for ease:

FLOURISH PLANNER (ongoing)

- Devote 15-30 minutes to tidying each day to stay on top of clutter/paperwork/keep spaces clear and organised.
- Early nights at least three nights per week (and stick to them).
- Drinking water every hour on the hour (you won't but you will drink more than you do now as a consequence).
- Exercise (classes, 15 minute bursts at the bottom of your BRAC, walking sessions, etc).
- Meal planning time. (I tend to do mine before I do my online grocery shop).
- Reminisce time – time once a week/fortnight/month to revisit happy memories.
- Laughter. (Make time to laugh. Schedule in a regular TV/ DVD/Book/Cinema/Night in or out/Trip to a comedy club).
- Deployment of signature strengths into social, work, family life/activities.
- Actions based on assessment of work/career/biz.
- Some FUN activities, some ENGAGING activities that harness your skills/strengths and some RELAXING activities including those which each family member LOVES to do. (See checklist)
- Some activities that you used to love when you were 10 or 11 years old.
- An activity that you've never done before that requires learning.
- Daily 5 minute mindful breathing exercise.
- Daily or weekly 15 minute mindful exercise from the Pick N Mix of Mindfulness list (stopping preoccupation and distractions on focusing on being in the moment).

- A block of time to make calls/send text messages/e-mails to those listed in my My Positive Peeps list and book in time to see them this week/month/year. Make it happen. Make my friendships flourish!.
- A block of time to lend support to friends.
- Regular meet ups of existing friends.
- New friend get-togethers / classes to meet new people.
- Daily noting down of positive traits of me and him/her in the 'I Love Us' worksheet.
- Fun activities that my other half/kids love to do, including more 'play' time.
- Time to do good deeds/acts of kindness.
- Time each day to record your gratitude in your gratitude diary/journal or jar.
- Daily, weekly or monthly affirmation/gratitude walks in 'your place'.
- Chores/calls/me-time AFTER the child(ren) are in bed, giving you more time to enjoy their childhood with them.
- Affirmations on a daily/weekly basis.
- Visualisation of goals having been achieved on a daily/weekly basis.
- Daily or weekly completion of MY JOURNEY worksheet.
- Monthly creation of Post-It Plan Schedule.
- Creating a daily prioritised to-do list of three to five daily tasks based on Pareto's principles. See printables below.
- Weekly planning – filling out the Ultimate Flourish Planner (see next chapter) based on 45-90 minute blocks of time.

Here's an example of what your FLOURISH PLAN may look like... here's mine:

The Ultimate FLOURISH Planner

	Monday	Tuesday	Wednesday	Thursday	Friday	Saturday	Sunday
7-8	6	6	6	6	6		
8-9	Language + Alpination / School Run	School Run	School Run	School Run	School Run	Family Time + REPACKING	PICK N MIX
9-10	BREAKFAST Social Media Posts	BREAKFAST Mindful E-mail Breathing	BREAKFAST Mindful Jog - Media Breathing	BREAKFAST Mindful Jog - Media Breathing	BREAKFAST Mindful Jog - Media	Play + Create + Repair	PICK N MIX
10-11	WRITING	CIRCUITS	WRITING	WRITING DANCE WORKOUT	Baby Jam DANCE WORKOUT	Papositive	Gratitude Walk ADVENTURE
11-12	WRITING	WRITING	WIGGLE	NEW PROJECT	NEW PROJECT	PERL / JUNK	carnival / picnic
12-1	WRITING	WRITING	WIGGLE	WIGGLE	NEW PROJECT	PICK N MIX	carnival / picnic
1-2	LUNCH (COMEDY TV)	LUNCH (Read) NEW PROJECT	LUNCH (COMEDY TV) WIGGLE	LUNCH (COMEDY TV) MENTAL TED	LUNCH (Read) NEW PROJECT	PICK N MIX	PICK N MIX
2-3	MEDITATE	MEDITATE	NEW PROJECT	TIDY / CLEAN	TIDY / CLEAN	PERL / JUNK	Resources :)
3-4	SLEEP / GYM TIDY / CLEAN	Mindful Meditation	WALK: Affirmations SHOWER Visualise	Library or meditate	Library Task Reminder ASSEMBLY	NEW ADMIN	creative / create
4-5	Smoothie	B-Football	SHOWER Visualise	B-Collection	B-Collection	PICK ADMIN	Relaxation
5-6 TEA	Read + Play	Play + Relax	Play + relax	Play relation	Smoothie	PICK N MIX	Relaxation
6-7	Chores + Cook	Friend Moment! + Question TEA	Chores + Cook TEA	Chores + Cook TEA	Chores + Cook TEA + REST ROOM	Chores + Cook	Chores + Cook
7-8	b + bed	B + bed	B + bed	B + bed	B + bed	B + bed	TEST FRIDGE MEAL PLAN + WEEKLY PLAN + TO-DO LISTS
8-9	WRITING	MARKETING	CLEAN (NIGHT) Read / Meditate Bath	MARKETING	NEW PROJECT	MEAL PLAN ONLINE SHOP or NIGHT IN FILM / COMEDY / WRITING	Read / Gratitude TV
9-10	WRITING	NEW PROJECT	NEW PROJECT	NEW PROJECT	MY JOURNEY + Gratitude Diary Read	FILM / COMEDY	FILM / COMEDY
10-11	Learning / Gratitude Diary Read	EARLY NIGHT	Read	Read	Read	Chores + Cook	EARLY NIGHT

Key:

- ■ ENERGY (Food / Sleep / Exercise)
- ■ PURPOSE (Using Strengths + Finding Purpose)
- ■ WORK (Using Strengths + Finding Purpose)
- ■ FRIENDS + FAMILY (RELATIONSHIPS)
- ■ WELL-BEING ACTIVITIES
- ■ All about B (mini time out's)
- ■ Household Chores + PLANNING

249

My flourish planner enables me to attain and sustain a really good quality of work/life balance. I work for up to 30 hours per week if necessary (pretty much full-time hours). And yet I am still able to be a full-time mum who does the school run and can give my daughter my full attention from the moment I collect her from school to the moment she falls asleep. During that time I am 100% mum. I also give myself time to reboot, to read and to relax. I take time to see and communicate with family and friends, to stay on top of paperwork, keep the house in a reasonably decent condition, feed my family, enjoy a variety of 'flourishing' activities and adventures as well as taking time to reminisce and feel/record gratitude for what I already have and plan for what I aim to achieve. I've even scheduled in time to record my enjoyment of the journey itself – a key component in flourishing that many people forget or don't have time to do.

If I had a 9-5 job (instead of a 9-2pm /8-10pm job) I would still be able to work around that all of these flourishing activities and time to be grateful, see friends, enjoy hobbies, exercise and so on.

I have colour-coded each part of the schedule.

- Green is for work (which I ensure plays to my strengths and enables me to pursue my passion and give my life meaning/ purpose).
- Red is for gratitude, flourishing and well-being enabling activities which boost positive emotion.
- Green is for energising activities.
- Turquoise is for social time with friends and family.
- Purple is for activities related to energy.
- Light green is my mummy time.

So you see, each pillar of well-being is covered.

Of course, sometimes life gets in the way and you have to reschedule that get-together with a friend or replace a flourishing activity with a work one due to a deadline and generally jig things around.

Juggling is a part of life. But, as long as you ensure that each of these areas gets adequate time, you'll be able to boost your well-being, enjoy your life more and reach your potential, as promised.

Your turn...

The Ultimate FLOURISH Planner

Monday	Tuesday	Wednesday	Thursday	Friday	Saturday	Sunday

Printable Quotes... to cut out n stick up

"The best thing about the future is that it comes one day at a time."

Abraham Lincoln

An Interview with a Flourisher

Matthew Robertson
MOMENTUM
ADVENTURE

Throughout this book we've learned that in this, our one and only life, it's vital to try to pursue our passion and purpose, fill our life and work with engaging activities where we play to our strengths yet step out of our comfort zone from time to time. We've learned the importance of building supportive relationships and enjoying the journey by noticing and appreciating what we already have as much as what we hope to achieve in the future.

I wanted to provide you with an example of someone who is living this kind of life and doing this kind of work; someone who is flourishing and, in doing so, enabling others to flourish.

Former climber, actor and TV presenter, Matthew Robertson, runs Momentum Adventure, a company he founded in 2005 which provides bespoke adventure travel to high net worth individuals with a future goal to enable all kinds of people from different backgrounds to go adventuring. We can't all make a living by taking people on extraordinary adventures of a lifetime (due to the complicated labour-intensive nature of the service provided and quality of its expert team, Momentum Adventure seems to have that market sewn up) but we *can* learn from Matthew's attitude, passion and drive. We can all seek out "food for the soul" and immerse ourselves in engaging activities as Matthew does and simultaneously strive to bring the best out in ourselves and in those around us.

Interestingly, in a way, Momentum Adventure mirrors this very handbook. Like this book, the company encourages people to go on adventures and engage in optimum quality experiences where 'flow' is likely to occur; it encourages people to work towards their ultimate dream destination but enjoy the journey along the way; to surround themselves with a trusted support network as they embark on their journey and return with an overwhelming sense of achievement and significant positive emotion.

Of course, as a flourisher, following his passion and pursuing his life's purpose came naturally to Matthew. Doing so led him to create a meaningful reality and a purposeful business.

"My vision and passion has always lay in the outdoors," Matthew smiles. "I find an incredible sense of peace being in the wilderness, in disappearing somewhere. I used to have a place in Chamonix and would disappear up into the mountains and just breathe, which is so good for the soul."

"My background comes from playing around as an actor in New York and heading to Up State New York to save my sanity and go climbing in the National Parks with my dog," recalls Matthew. After deciding he should probably get a 'proper and less sporadic job' and moving back to London where he met his wife (and fellow flourisher) Davina McCall, Matthew embarked on a mission to use his own set of strengths and skills as a climber, whilst pursuing his passion for the outdoors to create a business that would capture the essence of his open-air love-affair and enable people to enjoy the very experiences that he cherished so greatly (and then some).

A Positive Support Network

"I was climbing all over the world at the time and I thought, how can I take ordinary people and put them into extraordinary environments? To provide people who say 'if only I could' with the opportunity to actually make that happen." To do that Matthew needed to surround himself with "the best guys possible on the planet" from an ex-British commando and Broadcast documentary cameraman to a British triathlon champion and bush craft expert. And so he did, ticking the first flourishing box by creating a supportive network of positive relationships. The team are very supportive of one another and of anyone embarking on a trip with them.

"One of our biggest mottos is that we're only as strong as our weakest man," says Matthew. "If we're on a trip, if the last guy isn't strong, then we all make sure that we walk at his pace and ensure that he's OK."

"We all rely on each other immensely. And we're constantly bouncing ideas off each other. Every single person who is engaged in my business, whether that be a guide or photographer or associate, all have a passion for what we do. They love what we're trying to achieve. People buy into my business because of my passion to try to take the dirt out of adventure travel and make it exciting and aspirational. I'm totally passionate about the wild and the outdoors."

Certainly having a strong passion and focused vision makes it far easier to gain the buy-in of other people; to bring others into your vision and engage them to feel as passionate about it as you do. Indeed, purpose is a powerful enabler.

A Powerful Purpose and Meaningful Life

Matthew admits that it isn't easy to discover your true purpose in life and many people don't, but he didn't want to be one of those people who looks back on their life and wishes 'if only I'd tried that.'

"We grow up and go through school and I don't think anyone really knows what they want to do. Or maybe in the beginning you do, but then you get thrust into the real world working environment. Then you have a mortgage and a car and you get stuck. Everyone does, it's the nature of the beast. So we end up on this perpetual wheel of motion where we're chasing our tails until we're 60 and then you wake up and think... what the hell have I done with my life? What was it all about?"

Critical then to do your best to define your purpose as early as possible and embark on a mission to fulfil that purpose. Doing so is life-affirming. It gives you something to feel part of, something to embrace with vigour. Of course, that doesn't mean creating a meaningful life is easy.

While climbing and exploring were both within Matthew's comfort zone, setting up a business wasn't, particularly doing something that hadn't been done before. But, sometimes in life, you need to look at where everyone else is headed and go in the opposite direction. As Dame Anita Roddick once told me when I interviewed her for my first book, *The Small Business Start-Up Workbook*, "You've got to have something within you that makes you dance to a different drum beat to make you stand out from the rest and create your own thumb print."

"I chose the path less trodden," says Matthew. "Is it the most lucrative? At the moment probably not... but the potential now from the platform I've built is very exciting. What really excites me is the potential to touch more people."

As well as taking the less trodden route as a business and going in the opposite direction to others, Momentum Adventure makes a point of following that philosophy in each adventure it provides: "From Yukon to the Atlas Mountains to para-punting over the Gobi desert, if I can't make a trip extraordinary then I won't do it. You won't find a single trip that we do anywhere else on the planet, because we do it differently. Everyone else goes left, we go right. And there's a reason for that. If you take that path you won't be with the tourists and then you'll see that waterfall that the tourists miss.

That comes from a combination of experience and a preference to go in the opposite direction."

Harnessing the power of what you know and yet venturing out of your comfort zone, away from the crowds, that's the perfect blend when striving for success (its a strategy deployed by Steve Jobs, Richard Branson, Anita Roddick and other legendary business leaders.)

Pursuing your purpose often involves that dichotomy between utilising your core strengths, knowledge and experience *within* your comfort zone as well as stretching *outside* of your comfort zone by doing things differently so that you can shine and stand out from the crowd as you venture into the unknown.

"If you're going to make a career change, sometimes you've just got to go for it. For me, acting was lucrative but, wanting to do what I did involved taking a huge step in another direction into the adventure business. That was ballsy. There are no guarantees. But life is what you make it. If it's to be, then it's up to me. And if you want something badly enough, if you're really passionate about it and you've done your research, I say get on with it."

It's so much easier for people to stay within the security of their jobs that many people reach the end of their lives without having taking any risks, without having pursued their passion. But, as Matthew read in a book recently, "nobody ever got to the end of their life and wished they'd made more money; they just wished they'd travelled more and pursued their dreams in life."

"I've got a friend in Australia who is writing computer software and all he wants to do is be a photographer. He's made plenty of money so he could pack up his job and be a photographer, but he won't do it. Not everybody would," says Matthew.

"We don't live in the perfect world and we can't all sit at home with our family and hang out 24-7 and probably don't want to either, but for me that's what it's about: make a living but loving what you do and doing what you love. It's not the easiest thing to do, but it's worth it."

It's rather poetic that Matthew works in the adventure business because his journey to this point has been an adventure, primarily because it involved leaving his comfort zone, which is what Matthew believes adventure is all about.

"Adventure suffers from the Red Bull syndrome, where it's seen as 'extreme' or it goes the other way and, if you're not an extreme adrenalin junkie, you're seen as a soggy tent rambler. But I don't think adventure is any of that," explains Matthew. "I think adventure can be simply getting to work one day when all the tubes pack up. You'll end up going through London all different kinds of ways and you may see a shop or a path that you've never seen before and you suddenly start to experience something new. The simplest things can have the most profound effect. Just doing something differently turns it into an adventure. Adventure comes from leaving your comfort zone, that's when you start to experience again."

Stepping boldly outside of your comfort zone and exploring new things is stimulating and invigorating. Unfamiliar territory is adventurous and exciting. Conversely, doing the same thing over and over diminishes enjoyment of it. When you commit to be more adventurous and succeed in your endeavours, you boost your positive emotion and confidence tenfold. Even if you don't succeed, you gain confidence and learn by simply having a go; through trying.

Sourcing Engagement in Life and Work to Optimise the Quality of Experiences

Immersing yourself in experiences to optimise enjoyment by achieving a state of 'flow' is another way to flourish (as covered in Chapter Five). That's what Matthew did for many years as a climber.

"My brain runs at a billion miles per hour but, when I climb I find true peace, because you can only concentrate on the thing in hand. If you don't, you could end up in a world of pain. When I place a piece of gear and I'm thinking about the next move, I'm not thinking about taking the kids somewhere or needing to pay that bill or whatever it may be. I'm thinking 'I've got to clip that rope into here and then I've got to Mark [my teacher] safe, and I've got to do this bit'."

"When I get to the top of a climb I'm physically and emotionally exhausted," adds Matthew. "But there's a real sense of calm euphoria as you look over the scenery; it's incredible. That is soul food. It makes my heart sing."

Finding engaging activities which make your heart sing is a core part of flourishing. And you needn't scale a 2000 ft mountain to do it. Activities which enable flow whilst doing them and a sense of achievement when completing them boost well-being tremendously. Each moment makes up your life, so each moment is vital to maximise in terms of experiencing engagement.

And finding those moments of flow is what Matthew now enables others to do when they book a trip of a lifetime through Momentum Adventure. The activities undertaken on these trips are entirely absorbing. Much preparation before and concentration during them are required. Fishing in the wilds of West Vancouver Island or surviving in the jungles of Borneo are the epitome of engagement and are understandably intensely gratifying. That's what Momentum Adventure is all about – creating awesome experiences and memories that will last a life-time.

"For example, the Arctic is a very spiritual place," says Matthew. "And I'm not saying that from a religious perspective, it's just so peaceful that the silence can be deafening. And it's disarming taking a bunch of hedge fund guys out to the Arctic circle and watching them be totally bewildered. It doesn't matter who you are in the real world, out here nature calls the shots. This is where you're broken down mentally by mother nature. You can't control your environment and, once you let go, suddenly your spirit sings. And when people come back and reflect on what they've just done on the literal, physical and mental journey that they've been on, they're smiling from ear to ear," says Matthew.

"And that's my passion; that's what drives me, to give people these incredible experiences."

Clearly Momentum Adventure is not at all about extreme sports or getting an adrenalin fix it's simply about choosing life, it's about feeding the soul with memorable and engaging experiences. And that's something we can all do.

"Those experiences can be anything," says Matthew. "You just have to leave your comfort zone. I think the biggest challenge for most people is making the commitment to do that."

Enjoy The Journey
Once committed, the journey begins and Momentum Adventures, just like life's adventures, are all about enjoying the journey en-route.

"Interestingly I don't think it's ever the destination," says Matthew. "It's always the journey that is the experience. From the moment you get on the plane, to the walk to the base camp, to the trek into the wild for the first time, to setting up your tent or abseiling into a crevasse, it's always the journey and it's never the destination.

"Some people go to the South Pole and, after that initial high of getting there, when they look back at the trip they think about all the things that happened along the way; the preparation, and that bit when I was totally exhausted but had that cup of tea which got me totally warm in my tent while it was minus 60 outside. Little moments like that, little nuggets that you will always remember for the rest of your life."

Get Outside More
Although currently the trips provided by Momentum Adventure are tailored to high net worth individuals who "have the financial prowess to make something extraordinary happen," what Matthew

really wants to do is to touch more people. "My passion is to get more people outside and living the dream," nods Matthew.

That dream includes being more mindful about nature, soaking up its delights more frequently; just experiencing it, even if it merely means standing in a field pondering your plans.

"Simple things ...like, for me in the morning, I walk across the fields and just stand there and think about what I've got to get done in the day," says Matthew. "That five minutes of time on my own looking out to the fields and seeing nothing other than a few animals, that sets me up and I'm ready to go. Intimate experiences with mother nature are empowering."

In order to flourish we need to stand still and breathe (ideally outside in the fresh air). If we can do this, both on our own to find moments of peace and tranquillity, and with our families to embark on mini-adventures, then we are more likely to source that holy grail of well-being and find our flourish-ever-after.

"Time is the most precious commodity we have and we've got to savour every second," says Matthew. "I think unique experiences with your family are very powerful."

Devoting time and consideration to what you do with your family, planning adventures, planting seeds with them, going on bike rides, flying-kites – all of these outdoor pursuits lift us up together, unite us and, ultimately, engage us. The end result is relationships which flourish and a firmly-rooted sense of long-lasting well-being for the whole family.

Embarking on extraordinary adventures together help family relationships to flourish. Matthew is finding this as more and more father and son teams join his expeditions.

"Fathers who've been working their entire lives suddenly find that their kids are teenagers and they don't even know who their son is," explains Matthew. "I myself took my 10 year old daughter to the Arctic last year and we had such an incredible time in unique isolation. We had a great experience and, despite what people think about the Arctic, it's not all death-defying cold. Villagers in the Arctic circle live quite normal lives. My daughter never got cold and enjoyed every second."

In fact, Matthew is currently putting together weekend trips to the Arctic for families. Imagine that, popping to the Arctic for the weekend!

The Life-Long Gift of Enjoyment Through Engaging Experiences

Whether we spend our weekends in the Arctic Circle or circling country lanes on our bicycles, by taking time out of our busy lives to EXPERIENCE LIFE, we can enjoy the moment, create memories and then reminisce about the amazing adventures we've had, thus amplifying our enjoyment three-fold. By 1) anticipating the experience before it happens, 2) savouring it while it happens and 3) recalling it afterwards, we can achieve a level of happiness with staying power; an optimal level of flourishing.

As you've learned in this handbook, it's important to fill your life with as many autotelic activities as you can; I.e where the activity *is* its own reward, rather than doing it to gain some future reward. The acquisition of experiences and memories certainly makes for a far more enjoyable and meaningful life than the acquisition of superficial things.

Matthew agrees. "A lot of these guys that I work with buy the cars and the planes, but it's all temporary. The acquisition is the most exciting part and then it's dead. I think what we provide is memories and those memories last a lifetime. I don't think many people talk about the first time they bought a Ferrari or how fast they went," he adds. "At the dinner party they'd say, 'I just got back from the Arctic' and people would say 'wow! That is incredible.' *That's* what it's all about – experience! I'm in my 40s now and the need for positive experience becomes all the more evident."

And as time continues to zoom past at an ever-increasing speed, those who flourish are those who embark on adventures, whether big jungle-surviving Arctic-exploring ones or smaller bug-hunting kite-flying bike-riding ones; those who pursue their passions and purpose in life; those who stride out of their comfort zone into the great unknown, safe in the knowledge that it is better to try and fail (which is temporary) than to not try at all (which lasts forever). Those who flourish know that in harnessing their strengths and having a clear vision, no matter how alternative the direction is in which they are headed, they will achieve their goals and as they go through life, enjoying every step of their journey along the road less travelled.

Matthew's Lessons for Flourishers

- Get a supportive network of positive peeps around you. (See *Chapter 7 - Make Family Relationships and Friendships Flourish*).
- Disappear into your own wilderness from time to time. Get outside. Explore. Breathe it all in. Soak up the delights of mother nature. Experience it. Make it a habitual ritual to do so, whether it's every morning before you start work or once a week at weekends. Get out there.
- Embark on adventures. (See *Chapter 5 - Sourcing Engagement and Enjoyment for the Flourish Pick 'n Mix: 100 Well-being Boosting Activities Checklist*).
- Get out of your comfort zone, do something you've never done before. Dance to a different drum beat and pursue your passion.
- Harness your existing skills and play to your strengths and passions to find your purpose. (See *Chapter 4 - Create a Meaningful Life/Career/Business with Purpose*).

Visit Momentum Adventure
www.MomentumAdventure.com

Conclusion

We are healthier and more affluent than ever before; we have more choices and opportunities than we have ever had, and yet people tend to feel constantly frustrated and dissatisfied with their lot, filled with anxiety and worry or boredom and bitterness.

Why is that? Are we doomed to constantly want more than we have, to never be satisfied? Or can we change how we think and behave to enable ourselves and those around us to flourish?

I hope that this book has proven that much can be done. I hope that this book has given you the realisation that you can have more control over what happens to you and that you can make changes to boost your well-being, enjoy life more and reach your potential; to take the rough with the smooth and bounce back when things don't work out. I hope that this book has revealed to you that, rather than seek out happiness directly, you can build the five pillars of well-being by getting involved in each detail of your life; by seizing control over your relationships and what you do and experience on a daily basis in both work and in life. You really can cultivate more delight and bliss and achieve a sustainable level of well-being.

While comparison and the subsequent feelings of inadequacy are the norm, we can learn to shift our thinking away from continual comparison towards frequent gratitude. That pretty girl with the perfect husband may be struggling to have a family of her own; that wealthy guy with the dream house may be lonely; that woman with the perfect family may have been through a troubled past. There is no point in comparing or worrying as you never know the full story. If we can just stop that and start being more appreciative of what we have and of who we are, we can flourish-ever-after.

There's nobody quite like you and to some people you are the whole entire world.

People at the end of their life have told researchers that they just wish they'd let themselves be happier and not been so fearful of change.

How lucky are you? You're not at the end of your life, so you've got a second chance to make a real difference so that, when you do look back over your life, you don't have those regrets. Instead you can feel utter joy for how you have steered your wonderful life and all that you've experienced as a result of your stewardship and mastery. You seized it with both hands and cherished every moment. You bounced back and got on with things. You enjoyed the journey and oh what an incredible journey you had.

But what if you're not a positive smiley optimistic person? What if you do have a tendency to worry sometimes or be inpatient from time to time? That's still completely OK. If you have three or four out of five of the pillars of well-being you'll still flourish. You might not be high on positive emotion all the time, but you may still do a job that engages you which gives you meaning and you may still have fabulous friendships and relationships to support you. You may not be able to experience engagement as much as you'd like but you may achieve all kinds of goals. As long as you understand what is involved in flourishing and do what you can, you will still flourish more than you would have done without this knowledge. Research has revealed that, while hereditary factors and circumstances come in to play in terms of our overall level of happiness, 40 per cent can be boosted directly by our own proactive behaviours; by the choices we make as individuals.

I hope this book has gone some way to inspiring, informing, enabling and empowering you to flourish. If you make just one change... become more resilient, more able to see yourself positively, think positively or become more mindful or thankful as a direct result of reading this book, it was WELL worth me writing it and you reading it.

Books cannot wave a magic wand over your life or provide a fool-proof recipe for how to be blissfully happy. That depends on YOU, on your own efforts, on each moment you experience, on what you do and how you behave. But you can learn from what is presented among these pages about how to achieve happiness with staying power and what to do in order to boost your well-being and reach your potential. This book can teach you how to behave and respond to certain situations. And, while happiness as a topic has been somewhat over-published, flourishing is a far fresher concept. What I've aimed to do is what most books on these topics tend not to, to actually enable you, the reader, to make practical changes and MOVE FROM THE WRITTEN WORD to the *DOING* bit. To literally equip you with the tools you need to make the most of your one and only life. By filling this handbook with monthly tasks, daily actions and the GREAT BIG FLOURISHING PLANNER into which you can schedule stuff that will enable flourishing within your daily life, I hope you are closer to being a flourisher than you were before you picked this book up.

Please do let me know how this book has helped you. Because you are my reason for writing it.

E-mail me at cheryl@flourishhandbook.com

Also, please do join The Flourishers group on Facebook **https://www.facebook.com/groups/theflourishers/** to share with other like-minded individuals and readers of this book what you do/listen to/read... to boost your well-being and flourish.

You see, **I just want the world to cheer up.**

If you do too, please spread the word about *The Flourish Handbook* (www.FlourishHandbook.com).

Let's create a flourishing contagion and spread an upward spiral of well-being. You and I together...

Because life is a collection of moments and experiences which make memories. Make them count.

Wishing you a wonderful flourishing life from this day onward. Enjoy your life – it really is very amazing.

Cheryl Rickman
FlourishHandbook.com

PS: As someone who has bought this book, you can access downloadable colourful versions of the worksheets and printable quotes which appear in this book. To do so please go to http://www.flourishhandbook.com/the-flourish-handbook-worksheets and enter the password: flourisherworksheets

About The Author

Cheryl Rickman has been writing best-selling books on the big world of business from a small village in Hampshire for the past eight years. But recently, her purpose: to inform, inspire and empower people to start and grow their own businesses developed and she founded her third business, WiBBLE (Women in Business: Brilliant Local Enterprises) – a support network for self-employed women. It was then that Cheryl's writing journey ventured onto a different path as she noticed that many of these women, despite being brilliant, running their own little enterprises, were lacking in confidence and self-belief. Many were stressed out about the lack of time they had to enjoy life, despite the flexible nature of being self-employed. And so Cheryl was drawn towards a purpose that complemented her existing path, but this time to inspire, inform and empower people, not just in business, but anyone to boost their confidence and their well-being so they can achieve their goals and flourish.

What sets Cheryl apart from many writers in her field is that she has experience of starting up and running her own businesses; she has experienced adversity and tragedy having lost both her parents, her father just a couple of months before this book came to print. She has long followed her dreams, played to her strengths and pursued her purpose. She started her first internet business, aged 25. WebCritique was a web usability and content consultancy which she sold in 2005 to focus on writing. Clients included Microsoft, Business Link and Motorola.

Additionally, together with her partner, Cheryl co-founded ilikemusic.com (I Like Music) in 2000. During her time as Editor of ilikemusic.com, Cheryl spent seven years interviewing popstars and developing the business, living her dream.

Indeed, from popstar Katie Melua to rapper 50 Cent; from a death row prisoner to multi-millionaire business leaders, Cheryl has interviewed a variety of incredible people with extraordinary stories to tell.

Fifteen years after beginning her writing career, Cheryl continues to bring the stories of successful people to life. She's interviewed more than 100 entrepreneurs running businesses of all sizes, from one-man bands to large corporations; equally dedicated, passionate and insightful.

Founding and running two businesses from the age of 25 taught Cheryl about survival and enhanced what she was learning as a writer. This combination of knowledge and understanding gave her the confidence to write her first best-seller, "Probably the best book for Start-Ups ever written!"

Cheryl's first book, *The Small Business Start-Up Workbook* went straight to number one in the Start-Ups category on Amazon when it was published back in 2005. It has remained in the top ten of the best-seller charts in its categories ever since. Dame Anita Roddick kindly wrote the Foreword to that book.

Since then Cheryl has ghostwritten a number of best-selling books, including *Sunday Times* Bestseller, *Tycoon*, for Peter Jones of BBC Dragons' Den fame, and *Born Global* by Neal Gandhi of Quickstart Global. She also contributed to 1000 CEOs and recently helped Guy Rigby of Smith & Williamson to write *From Vision To Exit: The Entrepreneur's Guide to Building and Selling a Business*.

Her recent book, The Digital Business Start-Up Workbook has a Foreword written by the UK's Digital Champion, Martha Lane Fox and was published in April 2012 by Wiley/Capstone.

Today, alongside writing books, Cheryl continues to run WiBBLE and Flourish, taking groups of women on winter retreats known as Flourish Seaside Weekenders.

Cheryl lives near Winchester in Southern England, with her husband and their daughter.

4313648R00150

Printed in Great Britain
by Amazon.co.uk, Ltd.,
Marston Gate.